My father learned to drink and hide.
I'm learning all kinds of things.

WHAT ABOUT THE REST OF YOUR LIFE

SUNG YIM

a Perfect Day book
© Sung Yim 2017
The moral right of the author has been asserted.

Portions of this book have appeared in *The Margins, The James Franco Review, Contrary Magazine, Kweli,* and as a chapbook from Ghost City Press. This book was partially funded by a 2017 Oregon Literary Fellowship from Literary Arts. Several names have been changed.

What About the Rest of Your Life / Sung Yim
ISBN: 978-0-9836327-6-4
Library of Congress Control Number: 2017951345

Second printing May 2019

Cover design by Aaron Robert Miller
Photo by Jason Quigley
Perfect Day logo by Corinne Manning
Copyedited by Jessie Carver
Website by David Small

Printed by Worzalla in the United States of America
Set in Adobe Garamond and Hoefler Text

www.perfectdaypublishing.com

For Bryan, the last white man I will ever love.

CONTENTS

WHO IS THIS BITCH

I KISS MY BEDROOM WALL AT NIGHT. In the rigid darkness, I press myself up against the cold wall and glide my hands across its dimpled surface. Sometimes I close my eyes and picture Matt Damon. He's wet with rain outside a bar and having trouble lighting a cigarette. He doesn't tell me much but I somehow know he doesn't have a family. I have a family but I know how he feels—alone in the world. He doesn't say much, but he comforts me and I comfort him. I'm ten years old.

Sometimes I summon Winona Ryder circa *Edward Scissorhands*. She's wearing a soft angora sweater and always seems to be bathed in light. She's cold from being out in the snow, she's always out there just waiting and waiting but she doesn't know for what. Edward's retreated to his castle, leaving her lonely just like me. She's growing older. Her body is spreading and sighing itself an inch closer to death each day. She will always be beautiful to me and I'll always be beautiful to her even though I'm dumpy and short and growing breasts I don't know what to do with. I tell Winona I know this won't last forever but nothing does and we all die someday so I'd rather spend a second with her than spend forever without. Winona says she knows the boys at school keep asking if I'm 'a faggot or a dyke' and she knows they make fun of my weird pointy boobs but I'm the most miraculous thing to happen to her.

I frequently speak to the person in my bedroom wall. I am deeply attached to and wooed by the person in my bedroom wall. Sometimes I nuzzle my cheek against them and say, 'Oh, you're so sweet to me,' or 'I love you more than anything.' Sometimes I stretch out my arms to hold them and hiss, 'You're so beautiful,' or 'Everything's going to be okay.'

NO SUCH FUCKIN THING

TUESDAY NIGHT, RONNIE'S BRALESS in a white T like always. She sits with the covers over her bloated pink legs, blown glass pipe in hand and unlit cigarette between soft, gray teeth. The lights are dimmed and the TV's going real low. 'A friend needs something for cramps,' I say. 'They're real bad since this girl got a cyst removed the size of a grapefruit.' We pass a bowl back and forth while I stumble over how much I'm picking up.

There is no friend with cramps. Or at least, she's not who they're for. Ronnie traces one of the deep lines above her brow with a jerky finger, staring down the TV screen like it's a hole to put things in. She doesn't need all the bullshit. That's just for my own sake.

She limps off to the bathroom with the fifty I hand over. I ask if her knee's bothering her and she says for the last twenty years. When she limps back, I watch her slide the cellophane off her pack of Marlboro Reds, practice-smooth like her hundredth time undressing a man. She drops Vicodin in the cellophane wrapper and folds the top over as I chew my thumbnail. I ask if she's got Valium instead. Not to be a pain. I ask because maybe muscle relaxers are better for muscle cramps. I ask because I like Valium better. She picks up her lighter and singes the cellophane sealed without looking away from the TV.

'Hon,' she says, 'lemme tell you something.' She lights her long Marlboro and fills the room with it. 'There ain't no such fuckin thing as a painkiller. You ever take Vicodin after busting your shit? Pain doesn't go away.'

I remember falling down the stairs last month.

'Valium. Xanax. Vicodin. Hell, booze and weed. All they do is make it easy not to give a fuck. Just takes your mind somewhere else. Somewhere better.'

She hands me the little baggie. 'There's no cure for pain,' she says.

Before pulling all the way out of Ronnie's driveway, I tear the cellophane apart with my teeth. I drive around waiting for the warmth to find me. My room at home is four walls around a Pollock of neglect—disruptions of ash and sticky resin stains on Berber carpet, polyester fibers melted and cratered where a bowl was cashed before cooling. I'm not ready to go home to that. I duck in and out of strangers' cul-de-sacs, watching for something interesting in their windows, watching for movement, signs of life, telling myself there's something to find out here and I'm not just waiting for my chest to loosen farther than my breaths can fill. I'm ready to go home when it stops bothering me why I haven't yet. When I'm too fucked up to care about my mess of a room.

The TV's always on and on mute, the light's always changing. Televangelists, paternity tests, infomercials for a set of twelve knives. I watch the mouths flap soundless until the teeth break into pixels. I try to sleep scrunched to one corner of the bed, surrounded by papers and books and empty snack wrappers, by stacks of unread mail. I won't sleep so much as doze off, too scared to go to sleep on purpose, and the scrunching will help the bed feel safer, somehow. The crinkling of debris a comfort, somehow. It's the only way I know how to sleep.

I'm about to turn twenty. I don't want to die, but I've got nothing to live for. I've got nothing useful to say.

There's always a mess I'm too tired to clean up. I'm always too tired to do something.

I wash a bottle of Xanax down with milk.

There's always something.

There's going to be jazz in a ruined room. There's going to be a drunk boyfriend yelling racial slurs at the TV. He will be white-hot with rage, he will seem unreal, his anger stuck out of time like a folktale giant. He will say I smell clean for an immigrant. He will say spices stain his napkins and flare up his acne, he will say I'm good to look at for the fathers I have come from. He'll say I could be better, do better, he'll say I'm pretty when I'm not talking all that politic, he will break my habit of calling white boys who watch too many war movies. But white boys will keep calling. White boys will keep asking for dirty nothings in my first language. White boys will ask me to read their poetry, ask me to talk dharma, talk sushi, talk Stanley Kubrick, talk *so horny*, white boys will say they never made it with one of me and there's going to be jazz in a ruined room. The drugs will stop. The drugs will stop. The drugs caress my nerves in sweeping, tender breaths across the skin to teach me the feeling of body again. I'll wake into a movement of trumpet so sad I'll forget I'm by my-self. I'll forget the missed calls. I'll forget white boys crying for help, crying for spice, crying for rescue from their moms' buttered noodles and dinner table grace. There's going to be frosted glass jars of plum wine and my father talking Miles Davis because, he'll tell me, *no white man play this kind of sad*. There's going to be good ginseng, stained dark and bitter from the mountain earth in my grandmother's broth and the salt of my tears like the Yellow Sea splitting open under Truman's jets.

I'm about to turn twenty. My favorite movie must be Bres-son's *Pickpocket*. Or maybe Herzog's *Stroszek*. No, *Gummo*. *Kids*. Any bleak art-house vision of existential futility and transgressive shiftlessness. Movies that make me feel some-thing about not feeling anything, the titles just obscure enough to make me feel cultured and cool. I listen to a lot of Tom Waits and Captain Beefheart. I read a lot of Bukowski and Carver. I want to write like them. I want to sound like them, live like them, I want to be read and understood like them. I want my life's work to paint just as universally deso-late an emotional landscape as the works of these men.

I want to write terrible suns. Milk bottles like chilled lil-ies. I want to write about things falling. Gestures that try and fail, gestures that convey the unintended. I set the scenes of white men in their homes, ethnically invisible and brim-ming with nameless torment. I detail the minutiae of their lives—their rituals around cigarettes and therapy and mar-riage. I write these stories because depression belongs to the liquor-grated voices of working-class white men, paranoid anxiety and dependent neuroses to their white wives. That's what I've learned from *The Paris Review*, *McSweeney's*, *The*

Atlantic, Cannes and Sundance winners, from semester after semester of studying contemporary classics.

I write flannel and rain on cracked sidewalks. I write beaten-down Ford trucks. I write the flush of whiskey into a listless philanderer's cheeks as he thinks about a gun in his den. I believe I'm not allowed to materialize wholly myself on the page so much as in colorless tatters rammed through a sieve.

My mother will pull right up to the curb in front of a Ben & Jerry's. She will put the car in park and never turn to face me, and I will never find out what she sees out there, past the windshield, on that starless night. The engine will purr as I watch through a pane of glass, and through another pane of glass, some freckled white kids in canvas shoes sample all the flavors. My mother will say, 'You ruined our family.' The Pakistani franchise owner will grin and scoop and grin and scoop, tossing plastic spoons and grabbing new ones as the kids point out flavors with tentative gestures, hands held close to the chest, no intention to buy. How much money does he make, I wonder, does he get benefits, how many hours a week, what's he pay out of pocket for supplies around the shop. My mother will say it again. 'You ruined our family.' There will be another debt collector on the line in the morning to remind both of us. I will say, 'I know.' She will say, 'But I ruin your life.'

She will sit there and ask, 'Why you do like this?' She will ask, 'Why you do this drug?' She will ask, 'Why you always?' I will remember the heat of her hands across my face, the threats she spat at me in anger, the quiet house with no adults. She will say, 'That's Korean way,' and neither of us will buy the excuse, but we will both swallow its grave necessity. She will recall the day she wrenched me from the neighbor's house and her silence when I asked her what it was he had done to me, what it meant. She will recall the day she knew I had answered for myself, watching me unravel the *why* of rape, watching me condemn my body as liability, cuts growing across my forearms, knowing it was only one of all the reasons for my mess, blaming me when I blamed her, blaming herself when I could no longer, and she will say, 'You must forgive me.' She will drop the English to beg that I let God into my heart. I will have nothing useful to say. The kids will leave Ben & Jerry's without spending a cent. The radio will buzz white noise. I will never know a scene more American.

I start introducing myself with an Anglican name like it'll save me from the bold mispronunciation and scrutiny of well-meaning white folks. I cling to narrators and characters named Alice, Jerry, Carol, Peter in my writing like it'll cast a wider net. I glow when a teacher tells me I do a great job writing men. It never occurs to me there might be something wrong with feeling like I have to write men. Or that the men I'm writing are undeniably, invisibly, insidiously white.

I have no clue how to write about the people I know, love, and am. I have no clue how to make the words look right—even the word Korean, the word monolid, the word epicanthic, the fermentation, chili flakes, rock salt, rice, even my birth name, they look ugly on paper. They won't fit. The syllables like a rough chop, the terse layout of our names and places, they look ugly mashed flat through a Latin alphabet. They won't let my readers vanish into the feelings. The same restless feelings we all know to varying degrees: the isolation, the destitution of particularly interesting—and therefore troubled—comings-of-age. I can't write a serious story about Soo-Bin and Ki-Hong cracking open their first beer or drifting apart over a pregnancy scare. I can't write a story about them without mentioning where they come from, what their names mean, and without being asked for *more of that.*

I can't call myself 성애 without being asked for more of that.

Someone's always going to be asking. It will be more bearable than the assumptions. A straw-haired New Englander on TV will dump soy sauce in her kimchi fried rice. Some white tourist will write about 기분 as if *how are you* means something deeply mystical when asked in Korean. Or write about Eastern humility versus Western individualism. Eastern apology versus Western shame.

It will almost be a relief when someone asks, 'What's the difference between K-Pop and J-Pop?' 'Is everybody Buddhist there?' 'How do you tell between Korean, Chinese, Japanese?' Even though I have no conclusive answers.

There will be times when the questions fish deep into history. It will be like a long-forgotten splinter pushing through the skin. There will be the odd history buffs, white boys, Kerouac fans, long-time students of Daoism who will ask about comfort women and Japan, ask about communism in the North, ask about Seoul's embrace of Western commerce, ask why old women at the Korean grocery never say hello, please, or thank you. They will reduce intrusion to intervention, trauma to trivia, heritage to history, vigilance to hostility in their asking.

There will be white girls eating 반찬 without rice out of my mother's covered jars who tell me I always smell like fish.

There will be white boys pulling from my mouth to say 'your accent's not too obvious' as a compliment.

I will have so much to say, but nothing for them.

The trees are bursting plum and yellow, the sky a garish blue. I'm sticking my arm out the passenger side window to let it ride the wind. It's been a mellow spring. A friend is driving me to the hospital. She's crying.

She says, 'Don't do this to me.' I won't understand what or how for years. I'm still riding out the benzos.

My body is a busted bellows. I take long breaths that seem to keep filling and filling and hitting nothing. I'm here and I'm not. I'm laughing and I'm not. My friend turns up the radio to drown out her own crying, or my laughing.

I pass out in the waiting room while filling out intake forms.

I blink awake in cardiac, a butterfly needle in my hand and electrodes on my chest. Here I am. Wearing my heart on a monitor. I'm still stoned. My friend is sitting by my bed. She shakes her head and says again, 'Don't do this to me.'

I've got nothing useful to say.

The girl in the next bed over is crying noiselessly. The nurse stationed by our door suggests we pick something to watch on TV, nudging the remote our way. The girl asks if her mom has called. The answer is no.

I feel compelled to do something right for a change. There's always something to be done. I say to the girl, to make sure she knows, because I need to know that she knows, because it must be of profound comfort to hear in the starched womb of a hospital bed as she waits for someone to love her by showing up, 'You are, like, so pretty.'

I've got nothing useful to say.

There will be slanted glances across reading lists and mast-heads. There will be drafts where my name is Claire. Where my name is Joan. Where I don't miss the taste of jujubes and their red leather skins while the nurse asks questions. I will weigh themes and motifs, aspects of persona on the page by a rule of threes, wondering if Sung the Immigrant can frame Sung the Mess or Sung the Writer without eclipsing them. Like too much fish sauce. Too much chili paste. Too much ferment.

There will be more than this—there will be anticon-vulsants, dystonic reactions, excruciating loneliness, sleep as heavy as the moon. I will watch a woman twitch with seizures on a plastic sheet, begging me to close the door on her shame in long, winding moans. There will be wilted patients shuffling into the cafeteria for cups of applesauce, rocking in and out of sleep after sessions of electroshock. There will be a Turkish boy on Seroquel who's lost his grip on body and I will ask does he feel that draft, that scratchy carpet, that grainy powdered egg at every breakfast, does he like it, as he mumbles hello, thank you, and please, and white Midwestern nurses chalk broken thoughts up to bro-ken English.

There will be disgust. There will be despondence. Gulp-ing cold oatmeal without chewing as a tow-haired meth-head says, 'You speaky Chinee?' Waking to the creak of a door hinge as a nurse's eyes meet mine. She will count my breaths against the second hand of her wristwatch and though this is not the story, her eyes are green and mine are black as coal, the shadow of her profile will stand tall and jagged like a mountain range and I will vanish like a sunset, round and blunt and dimming.

This is not the story. There will be more. There will be more. There will be phone calls from my youngest sibling sniffling over static to promise kelp and taro upon my discharge. My brother's hugs cracking down to marrow as he calls me 누나. This is not the story but it is. There will be car rides with my mother full of heavy knowing-one-another, things unsaid, the tub of skin bleach that's left her pockmarked, tattoo ink greening beneath sparse eyebrows, tiny scalpel scars merging into crow's feet, things behind us, the story but not, things that sting to say face-to-yellow-face but must be written.

Usually I sit by myself on the school bus. I don't know anyone. Everyone else has friends. Everyone else is white. But one morning Emily Piasecki sits next to me. I am crying and I wish Emily Piasecki wasn't looking at me. 'What's wrong?' she says. 'It's nothing,' I say. She says, 'Why are you crying then?' and I tell her I almost missed the bus because I couldn't find my homework so my mom got really mad and hit me. Emily Piasecki puts her hand on my shoulder. She says, 'Your mom's not allowed to do that.' I'm crying. I ask what she means. 'That's against the law, your mom can't hit you,' she says. 'Didn't you know that? They can put your mom in jail.' I get quiet. 'Didn't you know that?' she asks again. I tell her it's no big deal. She says, 'Are you sure you're okay?' I say, 'Yes I'm okay.' Emily Piasecki and I don't end up being friends but sometimes I wish we had.

WHAT ABOUT THE REST
OF YOUR LIFE

After dropping out of high school, I start hanging with my friend Pat almost every day. He's a college dropout between jobs. An adult child of divorce living with his mom through the rest of his twenties after a shitty breakup that happened seven years ago. He has big brown eyes, sandy hair, a clean line of stubble, and that's about the only thing he ever keeps the same. He's always moving, driving somewhere, looking for something to do, always bored and so am I. Everyone else I know has shit to do. They're in school or working and before Pat starts calling me all the time, I lie in bed from morning to night smoking pot or knocking back fistfuls of Xanax and Vicodin because I hate being awake.

One day he calls up and invites me to dinner with someone he met at a yard sale. He's always meeting people at yard sales and coffee shops and movie theaters. It's weird, but nothing new. So we meet this guy named Bastian at a falafel place in Elmhurst. He's a skinny white dude with charmingly crooked teeth, around Pat's age. We grab a table out on the patio and talk over platters of hummus and kebabs.

Pat and I are over-sharing, talking about our worst hook-ups, breakups, traumas like it's nothing—that's just what you do when you're lonely. Bastian locks eyes and leans in whenever either of us speaks, but it's not intense so much as attentive and warm.

As we scrape the last of the hummus down our gullets with pita bread, sighing with ease, Bastian spreads an array of photocopied pamphlets in front of us. The headings say things like *Live Your Truest Potential* and *Meditation: The Path to Healing.* Bastian says, 'I used to feel that way. Like my life wasn't headed anywhere, like it had no *purpose.*'

Our napkins flutter in the breeze and birds jerk around in some nearby bushes. I don't know what to make of all this, but Pat gives a big, slow nod as he chews and looks over one of the pamphlets. He says, 'I guess meditation's a lot like prayer. Or therapy.' He'll look for anything positive to say and blames this people-pleasing trait on his parents' divorce. He fixes his sleepy brown eyes my way to gauge my interest. I'm pushing a single grain of yellow rice across my plate with a fork. The sun is setting behind Bastian, washing him out in this eerie glow. Dinner service is in full swing and all around us, there's intermittent chatter, silverware clattering, babies squealing impatiently, light bouncing off glass and plastic and metal. A traffic jam slowly loosens across the street, lone honks punctuating our pauses.

I shuffle through the pamphlets.

3 Easy Exercises to Center Yourself!

I don't know what that means. Center myself. Isn't my whole life just me already? Floating around, rootless? Isn't that *the* defining characteristic of suburban life? These insular clusters of homes winding into cul-de-sacs, streets named after dead rich folks and European cities that lead to nothing but a strip mall full of collapsing businesses—a mom-and-pop deli that turns into a George's Pantry that turns into a White Hen, then a 7-Eleven in the span of a decade? Nothing to do but bum around looking for basements to get wasted or hook up in, anywhere to go, trudging around sweaty in the summer, getting high just to make a trip to Dairy Queen feel worthwhile?

Exercise #1: Mirror Gazing

Sit or stand facing a large mirror. Stare into your reflection, allowing thoughts to wander in and out of your consciousness. Forgive yourself for drifting.

American cigarette brand Tareyton was created in 1954. Most brands today are packaged in light cardboard, but Tareytons come in soft sleeves of clear cellophane over pliable white paper over silver foil, like chewing gum. Two bold red stripes race down the front and above them, the name Tareyton in a black, tastefully tapered serif typeface. Each cigarette bears an emblem like an old English family crest in soft gray near the filter. Their longest running ad campaign featured smokers cheekily sporting faux black eyes beneath the tagline, *Us Tareyton smokers would rather fight than switch!*

The first time I bum one off Pat, I decide they're the only cigarettes I will ever smoke again. The long Tareyton 100's make me feel like a movie star. Soon I'm not a smoker so much as a Tareyton enthusiast. Due to their relative rarity, I have to drive all the way out to special Lake County tobacco shops to find them. Sometimes I actually call ahead to make sure they're in stock. Over the years, places have been phasing them out due to low demand and most shopkeepers ask me to repeat myself when I mention the name.

I have my pre-packaged justifications. *They taste better*—another ad campaign of theirs in the sixties boasted the unique design of their filters, a marriage of fiber and activated charcoal for smoother flavor. *They're stylish*—the minimalist packaging gives them the feel of a Truman Capote novel. When I'm low on gas money, I don't even bother keeping up my smoking habit. I could always switch brands, but the routine of the drive is part of their appeal. It's something to do. A reason to leave the house.

Sometimes I drive all the way out to Carpentersville to this employee-owned co-op called Woodman's where they sell these cigarettes. They're open twenty-four hours, so Pat and I walk in together after hot-boxing the car around half past midnight. The store is dead quiet, maybe three employees working the graveyard shift.

Woodman's sells stuff that seems stuck out of time, things you can't find in a Walmart. Pat points out a cereal called Blueberry Muffin Crisps that comes in a re-sealable plastic sack. I hold up a stick of Teen Spirit deodorant for him to sniff—the brand Kurt Cobain named a song after—and this particular stick of Sweet Strawberry makes Pat say, 'I would fuck an armpit like a vagina if it smelled like that.'

We browse novelty ice creams and sodas for maybe an hour, taking our shoes off to slide down the aisles until our highs start wearing off. Then we buy a bag of cheese curds, a stick of Sweet Strawberry deodorant, and a pack of Tareytons before leaving.

Some of these trips are more fun than others. We'll scramble past the frozen goods section, powered by manic jitters at two in the morning, giggling absent-mindedly. But sometimes we're all too aware of the fact that we're just passing time, postponing that moment later tonight when we'll lie awake smoking ourselves numb with the TV on until we pass out, terrified of the silence.

Most nights, I don't get to sleep until the sun starts rising and the birds are chirping.

One of those nights, Pat's beat-up gold Saturn pulls into my driveway. He doesn't need to honk or call for me to hear the tired engine rumbling through the basement windows and I don't ask why before running out there with my shoes untied. It feels like sleep can always wait. What's there to get up for in the morning, anyway?

The headlights shock my system awake like searing water. I trip over myself to slide into the passenger seat and buckle up. Pat is shuffling through a stack of CDs. He always picks the music. He says he just can't find something he wants to hear lately. He says that a lot and he knows it's not about the music and that *lately* is relative, he knows no song exists that will soothe him or even suit the kind of mood we're always in danger of falling into, that there's no precise name for this feeling but it's why we're always on the move at a moment's notice, he knows it's why I always pick up the phone, why we're always ready to drive twenty miles to a rundown Bollywood theater for cold samosas or to stalk the halls of someone else's church during evening services, so when he finally breaks down and picks a Smashing Pumpkins album, it's only because we're wasting gas in the driveway and he's restless. But he cranks it way up anyway.

He lights up his glass one-hitter and hands it to me. Smoke rolls out in thin sheets as we drive away from my street. The music's so loud I feel this grade-school glee, like *we're gonna get in trouble.*

I ask where he's taking us. 'To outer space,' he says.

Christ, the hokey bullshit we say when we're high. We laugh at how true we wish that were. At how nothing on Earth can excite or comfort us, how everything feels either alien or dead or maybe that's us. We drive down Mumford where the shinier two stories are, then past Pat's mom's house on Trailside Court, past all these boxy little houses built back in the seventies with aluminum siding that hisses in the rain, past worn trellises crawling with morning glories and ivy on streets we've walked most of our lives but never really known or loved.

Pat hands me this heavy tube as we turn onto Haman Street, where there's no outlet and the road winds off into the driveway loop of an elementary school that neither of us attended. This thing I'm holding feels like a stick of dynamite, heavy and wrapped in ham-pink paper. It feels dangerous. Pat explains that it's a road flare he found while riding around on his bike earlier. He doesn't say why he was out biking so late or where and I don't ask. We get out of the car and he points out a field behind the school building that dips into a grassy ditch by the woods.

'Kids play soccer out here in the summer,' he says. 'I used to lie in this field drunk in high school.' He sucks on that one-hitter like he really needs to believe that anything's fun when we're high, like we don't need reasons when we're high. 'Let's light this place up.'

It's so dense with blue darkness that I'm scared to move. Pat shuts the radio off, but leaves the car running like we might need to scramble back into it at a moment's notice, and the engine idles in a low rumble like thunder brewing.

We wade into the tall grass slowly. Pussy willows sweep against our bare legs as the swampy earth gives just enough beneath us to soak through our canvas shoes.

'Here goes nothing,' Pat says. He lights the wick of the flare and drops it. It sets off hot pink sparks as it rolls down into the bowl of the ditch. We hustle backwards and I expect everything to stop for a moment. I'm ready for the whole field to light up and bathe us in a haunting pink glow. I'm ready for the light to swallow us, consume everything, eat up all the sound and drown out the smell of grass and mud, wash everything out into a pink singularity, warm and suffocating like birth.

But it's a dud. The sparks fizzle away. It goes so quickly. The pussy willows and tall grass itch. The mud feels alive and festering. The mosquitoes have found us, buzzing violently in our ears.

Pat stares silently for a long while, like he's still expecting something to happen. Like he's giving this moment every benefit of the doubt. But when we head for the car, he leaves the flare sitting in the field. The engine's still running and no one is chasing us.

Exercise #2: Candle Meditation

Draw the shades and sit comfortably. Light a candle in the darkness. Look into the flame and watch its movement. Watch how it flickers with your breath. Allow your eyes to become unfocused. Take deep, even breaths as you do this for 5–10 minutes.

Bastian's home in Palatine, Illinois, is one of the oldest buildings on its street. The white paint has been chipped dark by years of weather. A wind chime of sea glass, feathers, and bird bones pings lazily with the breeze. This is an official branch of the School of Metaphysics, one of four in the state.

Every so often Pat and I drop by after office hours to have dinner, watch movies, and talk. Bastian is sautéing ground turkey as Pat washes spinach in the sink. The creaky old wooden house fills up with sizzling and the soft thuds of Bastian's wooden spoon. He reveals a little more about his life each time the three of us meet. He's originally from Connecticut. He hasn't spoken to his family in a long time. He dodges specifics a lot and tends to sum up years of stories with, 'It's been a long, winding path.'

Pat takes a break from slicing tomatoes to ask if I want to pack a bowl, but I tell him I don't feel like smoking. I'm not exactly sure why, but I'm starting to feel more uneasy about getting stoned in this place and around Bastian.

Bastian turns off the stove and lights a hand-rolled cigarette that he says he's trying to give up. His eyes are a soft gray and his voice waivers. He says it's his last vice and the School has gotten him off the worst shit. It's his next frontier. He wants to lead a life of *minimal waste,* a life of *clear goals and accountability.* He wants me to understand the meaning of life, too.

But I don't want the meaning of life. I want whatever makes Bastian so sure he knows it.

Pat and I exchange uncomfortable glances before he quickly turns back to the cutting board. We do the exercises, we hang out here, we read some of the pamphlets, but we don't know what to make of it. It's like we keep coming back to hang out with Bastian, like we're trying to get to know him, but we keep hitting a wall of taglines and pre-packaged phrases.

For the fourth time this month, Bastian slides a photocopied contract across the table. Today could be the day I sign up for weekly lessons in the language of dreams, astrology, and *purposeful living* for forty dollars a session. And after completing that curriculum, I could apply to the College of Metaphysics. They'd set me up in a chapter just like this to teach just like him. I could live in a charmingly old, off-white house in some sleepy suburb, too. Wake up with wind chimes gently dangling in the breeze, surrounded by crystals and pungent sticks of incense.

Bastian leans back in his chair and locks his cool gray eyes on mine. His plain white shirt clings to his chest. His dark hair falls across his forehead with no discernible shape to it. Every gesture seems to take an entire era, carefully determined and quiet. There's no inertia to him. He moves like sludge. 'Sure, you're okay now,' he says. 'Killing time every day. But what about the rest of your life?'

I look behind him at Pat. I look down at myself. Our loud floral print shirts, wild bursts of color in everything we own, our dirty hair, our muddy shoes, our frenetic gestures. I think about laughing so hard it aches. I think about the long pauses we take in conversation, the easy fluid energy. The crying. The tantrums. The pill binges.

There's got to be something in the middle.

'I don't have money like that,' I say to Bastian. I slide the contract back across the table and decide I'm never coming back here again.

Exercise #3: Record Your Dreams

> *Keep a notebook by your bed. Record the date and time before closing your eyes each night. Write*

everything you can recall about your dreams first thing each morning. These recollections may be fragmented at first, but this is an acquired skill. Be patient with yourself.

It's been years since I've seen Pat. I can't really say why we stopped talking but that's how things are. There was no big disagreement or goodbye. Your time with someone can peter out like that. Things change.

It's three in the morning. I am naked in bed next to my husband and dog. I can't sleep. I am furiously Googling a life I almost lived and the people I almost lived it with.

Some things stay the same.

I find an old blog of Pat's. One of the posts says: *I once knew a girl with armpits like a Modigliani painting.* I think of those trips to Woodman's and how we kept going back so he could buy more Teen Spirit. Another post says: *I don't want to sleep, I want to run around and play.* It's dated around a time neither of us was sleeping much. The summer when everything was sticky with sweat and resin and we spent most of the time getting high in a church parking lot, spit-balling things to do, new places to eat. Another post from the year before we met: *Is anybody reading? Are you out there?* No reply.

I wonder who he was hanging out with back then. I'd seen him sauntering around the neighborhood in a spray-painted denim jacket before we met. He didn't look like anyone else, he didn't look like he lived in the suburbs. And he looked lonely. He'd pop up at the one record store we had in town and I didn't know his name for the longest time.

I don't know where he's been at but I have this feeling like he's still at that old house on Trailside Court trying to blow pot smoke out the window so his mom doesn't bug him. Like maybe if I pull up there and knock, he might answer and we could go on an adventure. But what's the endgame if I do track him down? And then what?

So much life has happened since I last saw him or the old schoolhouse that sometimes I forget I ever did. I got into a writing program at an accredited four-year university, got into a relationship and out of one, slept with four people for stretches of time spanning from weeks to years, met and married my husband. We got an apartment, got sober together, lost our oldest dog, we've cried and fucked hundreds of times and our one-year wedding anniversary is coming up. I'm graduating next semester and putting together my portfolio for grad school. We have years of plans in the works and for the first time in my life I know what I want and where my life is going but there are still nights I can't sleep.

I type into my search bar: *school of metaphysics palatine.*

Their official website says the institution was first founded in 1973, its headquarters located in Windyville, Missouri. Most of their branches are located throughout the Midwest (one in Texas), offering workshops in meditation, dream interpretation, and self-actualization—I have no idea what that's supposed to mean.

The website yields little concrete information as to the nature of their coursework beyond these terms. The distantly optimistic descriptions of the school's teachings feel eerie and vaguely cultish. 'The Purpose of the School of Metaphysics is to accelerate the evolution of humanity by ushering in Intuitive, Spiritual Man,' the site's *About* section reads. They promise to help you become a 'Whole, Functioning Self, not dependent on any person, place, or thing for peace, contentment, and security.'

My husband suddenly snorts in his sleep. I look up from my laptop's glowing screen as he shifts away from me to breathe easier. But his hand stays on my shoulder. His hand is always touching some part of me no matter how much he tosses and turns.

There will always be nights you can't sleep, when the room goes dead with silence in the dark and you look around thinking all these clothes, books, pieces of furniture, all this *stuff* is replaceable, like you don't need anything, nothing means anything really, and you're hopelessly bored, feeling weightless like a helium balloon fighting its tether in a storm, absurdly fucking bored in the dead of night so why not hop in the car when you should be sleeping to drive off without a plan? Like what's the difference if you grab all your cash to *go somewhere* and never come back? There will always be nights like that. Nights you find a blog post an old friend wrote that says: *I was just reading somebody's journal. Does that make me a bad person? I guess if it's public, then it isn't private* and you feel exposed though no one's looking at you. When you think maybe it's a big sign, like you were destined to read it at that exact moment when you were feeling exactly this way.

I wonder, would Pat have read my journal if I kept one?

Is that question why I don't keep a journal at all?

There will always be nights like this. So you lie down. You close your eyes as the birds start chirping and flitting around, as the sky ripens a cool blue.

You need your mother. Your mother beats you. Translation: You need your mother to beat you. Your mother loves you. Your mother beats you. Translation: Sometimes love looks like this. You look for a love that looks like this. You love your mother. Your mother hurts you. Translation: Pain becomes a beautiful thing.

The year before I turn twenty I'm compulsively trolling fetish chat rooms when I meet a series of terrible men from out of state. They want me to cry on the phone for them while they tell me what to do to myself. They call me pig. They call me whore. They sometimes make me cry for real.

I don't know why I do it. Maybe it feels good to feel bad. I feel *something* when I talk to these men. Something.

I can't stop. I keep picking up the phone. No one else wants to talk at 3:00 a.m.

The year before I turn twenty all of my friends have jobs or they're at school. I'm taking classes at a community college, but only part time. I reply to Leo's ad on Craigslist. He says all he wants to do is watch a movie and smoke some weed. If anything else happens, that's cool. He's shorter than I expect. He moved here from Croatia to attend college and speaks with a thick accent. He has big, bulgy ice-blue eyes and thick lips. I've always been attracted to people like him, misfits and foreigners. Not exactly beautiful but sexy. Not exactly the cultural ideal but peculiar.

I sleep over at his place at least three days a week. We don't put any label on it and truthfully he's too old for me. Even more truthfully, he's one of the youngest guys I've been with. I keep asking him if he loves me, telling him I love him, and he keeps telling me of course he cares about me but he doesn't want to get too attached after his last heartbreak left him unable to function for years. He says, 'Maybe one of these days we'll go out for dinner.'

I talk it up to everyone. He loves me, I know he does. I say that all the time but honestly I'm not sure I know what love is. I'm secretly unimpressed by his taste in movies and find it kind of weird that he uses lube like massage oil. But he says maybe one of these days we'll go out for dinner and we're fucking so he has to love me and I kind of like him so we have to fuck.

It's a mess and maybe he does actually want to *be with me* in the way I'm desperate for but I give off nothing but red flags—I gnash Xanax like M&Ms, I over-text, I over-share, I fuck with my eyes closed and kiss with my eyes open, I cry at the drop of a hat.

Every once in a while he says he worries about me. He holds me very close at the doorway each morning, for minutes at a time. His long, slow breaths flood me with a different kind of calm than the drugs. And it hurts. When he lets me go, he says *take care of yourself* in a hoarse quiver that makes me wonder if I know how to do that. I often cry on the drive home.

I'm unemployed. I've already sold all my records and DVDs. I start running out of drug money. There's no conscious part of me that admits to being an addict. Years from now I'll still have those moments where I truly forget all this shit, forget all the binges and all the days spent achy and throwing up in bed from the shakes. Years from now I'll buy a huge stash of Xanax and tell everyone I'm just *responsibly self-medicating* and before I know it I'll start popping two, three, four at a time, staying up until my husband falls asleep just so I can take a bunch and enjoy it in the dim silence. Years from now I'll spend Thanksgiving hunched over the toilet in a bathrobe, sweaty from detoxing. But I don't see any of that coming yet. All I know is I'm running out of drugs and I want more. *This is just a thing I like doing,* I tell myself, like it's no different from knitting or collecting records. So I put up a new ad on Craigslist, this time for sex work. I start peddling ass, meeting strangers at their apartments to jerk them off and swallow their cum for wads of cash, not even thinking about it really. Plenty of clients hit me up before my ad gets flagged. I make something like three thousand dollars in a matter of weeks and blow it all on downers.

One day a prospective client messages me. He's asking about my services one minute and interrogating me about my life the next. He says he knows my father. He says I need to stop doing this kind of thing. I'm shaken. I don't know what's going on but it's deeply uncomfortable. I stop responding to the emails and pop a few more Xanax. I get a text from Leo asking if I fuck for money. I deny it at first but he says his coworker saw my ad.

'It's not that you're fucking other people but how you're doing it,' Leo says. It's not like he expects fidelity from me, he adds, after all we never agreed to be monogamous and we're not even anything so this doesn't mean we have to stop seeing each other but things have to change. He tells me he was thinking of taking me to his office New Year's party but there's no way, not now.

We keep spending nights together for about a year, but we never do go out for dinner.

Things change, but they kind of don't.

So I'm twenty-six and the man on the phone says, 'You're an ugly cunt.' He says, 'Say it.' I say it. He says, 'Gooks are only good for serving the superior white man.' I don't say that white men like him are only good for their paychecks.

I hate him, but I get wet.

It's nothing unusual.

The body lies.

PAINT BY NUMBERS

POINTILLISM, A TECHNIQUE OF CREATING a cohesive painting through the clever arrangement of dots, was developed as a means to bring discipline to the loose, intuitive aesthetics of Impressionist art. Up close, the full context of a pointillist work is lost in an abstract array of freckles.

The first time I meet Mr. Grossman, it takes me a moment to realize why he doesn't want us touching his things.

After I've plowed through a long post-holiday line of returns and exchanges, here comes this older guy. He holds up a cautionary palm when I reach for his tall stack of magazines. He tells me to keep my hands to myself. He wants me to scan his items without touching them. I have no clue what he means until he tells me to take the scanner out of its plastic holster.

In the middle of the transaction, he mentions coupons. He digs a crumpled piece of notebook paper out of his pocket and reads me a code. We are so close to locking up for the night. I've only been working here for a few weeks, so I defer to my store manager Sarah who explains that we're really not supposed to take handwritten coupons as these codes are one-use-only, but she'll make an exception. Sarah is a master of taut, red-faced smiles. When Mr. Grossman notices her sniffling and coughing, he flinches. She apologizes in a sing-song voice that she has a *terrible cold,* at which point he demands that she not touch anything, not do anything more. He requests that I finish up, and we explain that only Sarah can approve the transaction coupon. He no longer cares about that. All he wants is for Sarah to back away.

We don't finish the transaction until fifteen minutes past close. He pays with two separate gift cards. Sarah and I watch with glee as he fumbles to squeeze a glob of sanitizer into his palm with bags hanging from both arms. He drops one of them, spilling its contents across the tiles. He hangs his head.

Mr. Grossman stands before the register, staring down at his magazines. He must be contemplating the futility of his efforts to mitigate disaster, the acute crisis of having had no disaster to mitigate.

I fidget with the stack of plastic bags behind the counter, trying not to look at him. I know exactly how it feels to live one's whole life thrashing blindly against the invisible and looming. The familiar emptiness of standing there with nothing left to do but admit to yourself that despite all your efforts, you're not in control.

I collect nervous tics like it's a hobby. First it's nail-biting and picking ingrown hairs, it's making sure my car windows are exactly parallel and that the thermostat is set at an odd number and that the radio volume is always a multiple of five. These are the small pleasures I allow myself between binge-purge sessions. When the picking and gnawing and fine-tuning prove themselves so uniquely satisfying that I crave more, to pick all the way to the bone, I allow myself to eat an entire box of something and forgive myself by puking it up.

In workshops, professors ask us *who we are on the page*. We chart our 'magical threes'—three aspects of self to build one rounded persona, three distinct motifs to weave through our narratives, three examples in each elaboration. And inevitably, *the mess* is someone who shows up in each of my essays. Sung—the student, the immigrant, the mess. Sung—the friend, the addict, the mess. Sung—the survivor, the child, *the mess.* I'm living one of those narratives in an idling Honda when my mother looks straight ahead and says, 'You've ruined our family.' When I move in with an abusive drunk who's way too old for me. When I cringe at loud noises, constantly forgetting what day it is. I'm a mess, calling the suicide hotline again and again when the operator berates me for going back to him—'Why should I help someone who's just going to waste it?'

I'm Sung—mess in recovery, cashier in student loan debt—when Sarah calls Mr. Grossman 'a total weirdo' after locking up behind him, and I'm silent. When another coworker mumbles under her breath that he 'probably just has OCD or something,' and I'm silent. I'm Sung—magical thinker, lapsed Presbyterian—warm with the smear of guilt like a big, red stain as I pick apart my unwillingness to defend him. Mr. Grossman's mental health issues are perfectly understandable, but did he have to be so rude about it? Did he have to make his problem everyone else's problem, too?

Two summers ago—I'm running up and down Pauly's townhouse with a can of Lysol in one hand and a roll of paper towels in the other. I don't remember what it is this time.

No, I do. It takes a minute. It always takes a minute.

Pauly has a strict regimen of drinking Crown Royal all weekend starting as soon as he gets home on Fridays. Five fifteen sharp. He has precise expectations: one jigger of whiskey on the rocks, topped off with cold water. He's never shy about pointing out when there's too much of this, not enough of that. Three ingredients and I never seem to get it right.

Friday night, he's sniffing my neck and saying I smell like flowers. He says he can smell me in a room I've been in like I'm an exquisite trick of the light. Come Sunday, he wakes up with a zit. The skin cream for his psoriasis tends to aggravate his acne, and his acne medication tends to cause psoriasis flare-ups. The booze doesn't help. But he's convinced it must be the shea butter lotion I've been using. The one that smells like flowers. He's screaming about essential oils and what they do to his pores. He punctuates sentences with 'my house' a lot. His rant is filled with phrases like *that filth*, *my rules*, and *fucking twat*. His rant spins psychotic, it goes from territorial rage to delusional paranoia. He says I've let the devil in his home, I've been whoring around with Satan. He calls me Lucifer's puppet. Every time I try to open my mouth he snaps, 'Satan is the father of lies.'

He hands me the disinfectant and tells me to wipe off every surface I've touched since I've started using that lotion. He throws out all my bath products and replaces them with harsh, orange, antiseptic versions—Dial bar soap, Dial liquid soap, CVS brand moisturizer. It's not about what's logical, but what's familiar.

Eventually he's calm enough to eat something instead of screaming obscenities and calling me the devil. I tell myself he's a sick man and he needs me. He tells me the same thing and I can't remember who started saying it first.

On my commute home from the bookstore I find myself negotiating a new shade of truth—Mr. Grossman, favorite customer. Mr. Grossman, under-medicated and misunderstood. Mr. Grossman, the slashed and sculpted version you'll hear from Sung—short story writer.

Actually, Mr. Grossman's kind of an asshole.

One night, he saunters up right at close, demanding that I ring up four books in four separate transactions, redeeming each one with the same exact coupon. I have to get Larry, the manager on duty that night, to explain with some higher authority that we can't honor his request. On top of that the register won't even read the code but Mr. Grossman is chillingly calm about it—eye contact steady, voice unwaveringly clear and pleasant as he explains that he doesn't even need these books, that he's actually *doing us a favor.*

Larry's a soft-spoken guy with a beard and ponytail who comes to work in cargo pants covered in dog fur. Authority is something he exercises begrudgingly. This is his first time face-to-face with Mr. Grossman, who keeps asking the same question—*why not*—while Larry asks him to please just respect his opinion on the matter. 'The booksellers who let you use that expired coupon previously *were wrong* and *I'm sorry,* but I don't make the rules.'

It takes us an extra half hour to get through closing duties that night. Once the magazines are straightened and misplaced books are put away, I apologize to Larry for the trouble without even being sure why. He pauses and chuckles politely, like I've told a bad joke. He tells me not to worry about it, assuring me that it wasn't my fault. There's this strange and unspoken understanding between us that I need to hear this.

Pauly's on the phone, trying to fix a billing issue with the cable company. I commit to memory the tight-lipped way he enunciates *cus-to-mer ser-vice,* and, after a sip of beer, *bil-ling* to the automated system. I will write another poem tonight that my professor will slash through with ink, writing *too vague* in the margin.

While on hold, Pauly mutters cusswords and fiddles with the remote control. He bounces his leg with nervous energy. When someone picks up the call, he reverts right back to breathing-quietly-through-the-nose Pauly. Hey-how-ya-doin Pauly. It's the version of him I see at office parties, when he parades me around in the dress he sent me out to buy. For the bulk of the call, he gives a lot of steady commands in such a calm tone that he almost sounds like he's asking a buddy for a ride home. 'Come on. Just this once. *Why not.*'

I can't recall at what point he starts screaming, but we end up with free cable for that month and premium channels for the next year.

Next billing cycle, I'm the one on the phone while Pauly's at work. While the hold music plays, I scroll through his daily emails where he tells me not to forget the groceries tonight, and that we really need to start pinching pennies with this cable problem going on. Turns out the premium channels weren't free and we're being charged extra for them. Pauly is furious. And, by extension, as long as I'm home alone with no one pressing me into passivity, so am I.

If I do this, then aren't we golden? Haven't I been good? If I fix this, won't my poems start making sense again?

The customer service rep is calling me ma'am. I'm shuffling Pauly's papers into neat stacks and shouting that this is bullshit. I didn't ask for this. You promised something and delivered a shitload of hassle. I'm shouting myself hoarse as I pace up and down the house, washing a dish here and loading the dryer there. I'm shouting as this man explains in a weary voice that there's nothing he can personally do. I know that. I know.

He gives me his supervisor's number and I say I'm sorry. I'm so sorry. I hang up.

I start dinner. I hate myself.

Mr. Grossman comes in every Sunday night around seven thirty, wearing exactly the same outfit—jeans and a mossy gray sweatshirt with the sleeves rolled up. In damp November, he lumbers through the café with rain-dappled hair. He stands square in front of the magazines on the coldest day of January, the skin of his forearms rubbed pink with frost. At eight o'clock, as my manager announces over the intercom that the store is closing, Mr. Grossman surveys the checkout line and hangs back until the last customers take their leave. He looks up and smiles when I hold up the scanner.

He says, 'You've got it down pat, huh?' He shows me the barcode on each item and I scan them from where I am. I apologize when my cash drawer springs open. There were forty-six cents left on his gift card. Mr. Grossman doesn't get upset. He holds out his palm to receive the coins without protest. He notes how funny it is, though—after all these precautions, like buying gift cards online just to avoid touching money and other people, look what happens.

'Y'know the worst thing you can do is touch money,' he says. He shakes his head with a dry, hissing laugh. 'Maybe I'll get over this germophobia thing, one day.'

Seeing a Seurat, seeing *the* Seurat—you know the one—can be frustrating. On the one hand I don't understand what's so compelling about a bunch of expressionless figures standing around at a park. Part of me resents the notion that a meticulous process can indiscriminately breathe life into something so joyless and banal. On the other hand, Cameron from *Ferris Bueller's Day Off* is a big part of all of us. Looking into the painting from a cynic's perspective will enchant and enrage you because it beckons a special kind of perception that takes work, and you are then moved, begrudgingly, by your own effort.

It's strange how pointillism—intended to refine the focus of an artistic movement—led to the division of tones into dots, refracting the act of looking into the work of seeing. It's funny to me in a way I feel I've misunderstood. This is the kind of ex post facto irony I sniff out when Mr. Grossman's gift card closes out and my cash drawer opens. I wonder if a punch line has gone over my head.

Some workshop professors will say you can write the same essay a hundred times because there's no such thing as a single objective narrative in real life. Truth doesn't come in shades so much as numerous specks of one indisputable, collective experience that no one has the distance to see.

Like Seurat furiously devising his theories and techniques, building lawful connections between colors to other colors and dots to other dots and dots to colors to dots, some part of me needs a tidy pattern. I am tempted to reframe the flashing atrocities of memory and imbue them with significance—to stave off the cold trickle of fear like germs in the abstract.

If Mr. Grossman is my favorite customer, then Pauly was just broken and I didn't have the fix in me. If I can forgive him, then the world can forgive me.

Here's something I've never told anyone.

The year before we move to America, I have a strict Catholic teacher who is always wearing a rosary and gray skirts down to her ankles. She has a neat haircut and a short, righteous temper. She hates stupid questions. I've been punished more than once for speaking out of turn or leaving toys out of the box after recess. Sometimes she whacks us with a ruler or gives us big metal pails of water to hold straight in front of us while standing in the hall. If she catches our arms sinking to the floor she whacks us with the ruler again.

One day I have to pee during class. I'm so scared of making her angry but I raise my hand. She gives me a stern look for interrupting and tells me to be quick. I can't remember where the bathroom is. I wander the halls, but this building is huge and its doors are all the same. I can tell it's already been too long so I go back to class and ask where the bathroom is. My teacher points and barks some directions but I can't follow them. I wander some more without finding the bathroom so eventually I sit back down at my desk and pray school will be over soon.

I feel stupid. I should have figured it out. School started weeks ago. How could I not know where the bathroom is. What's wrong with me. Everyone seems to ask what's wrong with me. I can't hold it anymore but I'm too scared to say anything. I pray no one notices when I wet myself.

Trauma doesn't occur in a vacuum. You don't outgrow it with time. It grows with you, even if the growing goes all wrong. It's like breaking an arm and never putting it in a cast. You're bigger, but the bone is still broken. Maybe there's a throb of pain once in a while. You can't just stop using the arm. The more you use it the more it tears and contorts. You get clumsy. You break more limbs. Even if you see a doctor now, there's no going back to the beginning.

My freshman year of high school my friends say I look so thin, in a good way. My therapist says I look sick. On New Year's Eve my boyfriend takes me by the hand and the next thing I know, I'm in my bed mouthing the word 'no.' I don't know how to say it out loud. I say 'wait' instead. He doesn't. I say, 'I'm not sure I want to.' But he is. He really, really is.

OH MY OH CHICKEN SOUP WITH RICE

MRS. SNOW IS THE OLDEST WOMAN I KNOW. Her breath always smells like a cross between steamed peas and a sneeze. She has hair the color of straw in the sun, cut bluntly at the forehead and shoulders like a ragdoll's. She keeps a shawl draped across her desk in case the room gets chilly. Every afternoon at school, she whisks me out of the room for my English lessons.

I'm doing this worksheet where I'm supposed to connect a phrase on the left to its respective contraction on the right, dragging a pencil line from *I am* to *I'm* and *cannot* to *can't* on a sheet of paper. There's a cartoon dog sitting in the corner for no reason.

Mrs. Snow says I look bored. I don't answer her because I don't what the word 'bored' means.

'How about we learn something new today, then?' she says. 'Something fun. Like rhyming.' She explains to me what rhyme is—when two words share the same vowel, like dog and fog, hike and bike. We went over vowels a few weeks ago.

Mrs. Snow picks something out of her bookshelf and sets it down in front of me, right on top of the worksheet I've rushed through in the hopes of leaving sooner. My pencil rolls past the edge of the desk and rattles against the floor, but we don't reach for it.

She points to the author's name. 'This is a book by Maurice Sendak. Can you say that with me?'

I stare quietly. Mrs. Snow flips through the book, turning to random pages to show me glimpses of cross-hatched illustrations.

'Mau-*rice Sen*-dak. He wrote all the words. And he drew all these nice pictures,' says Mrs. Snow. 'He's one of my very favorites.'

I watch her flip through the book as if she's looking through an old photo album. She reminds me of my grandma sometimes, when we're having fun. They both have this private way of smiling, of adjusting their glasses and watching me play. It makes me wonder what they're thinking about that's so nice. Mrs. Snow's mooning eyes make me want to know what's so great about Maurice Sendak.

She sets the book back down in front of us. I read as she sweeps her finger under each word. 'Sipping once, sipping twice, sipping chicken soup with rice.'

This is the first poem I've ever read.

In the cafeteria one day this blue-eyed little girl named Emily scrunches up her nose when I open my lunchbox.

She asks, 'What *is* that?'

We call this 주먹밥. 주먹 meaning fist, and 밥 meaning rice, as in rice shaped with the fist. Or rice the size and shape of a fist. There's this toughness about the name that I feel describes my mother perfectly.

My mother, who took the time to cook a pot of rice and dress it with sesame seed oil, vinegar, salt, and a smidge of sugar. She tossed the rice while it was still hot, so the sugar and salt would dissolve more easily. She did this with bare-handed poise, distributing seasonings between each scalding grain, careful not to crush them. The skin of her hands is tough and thick after years of handling heat and spice.

When Emily scrunches up her nose and asks *what is that*, this is what rushes through me. But there's no word for *all this*. There's no word for watching my mother form a shell of seasoned rice around chopped salmon and rolling it in toasted sesame seeds, no word for learning the right amount of pressure to pack without squishing through years of repeated tradition, no word for even the simplest of go-to meals that have been passed down to me with no verbal instruction, no word for the way my mother licks her thumb when she slides a single perilla leaf from the stack like turning a page of a book, or the sound of it when she lays it down at the bottom of my lunchbox to keep the rice from sticking, no word for the kinetic and olfactory language of caring for one another.

But at home, we call this 주먹밥. 주먹 meaning fist, and 밥 meaning rice. I haven't learned the word *fist* yet, not that it's of any use when Emily asks *what is that?*

I panic. I know what a fist looks like, but I don't know what it's called. They're for punching. I tell Emily I'm eating *punch rice*.

'Punch rice?' she says. She arches an eyebrow. My body seizes up with embarrassment and I start giggling uncontrollably. This might be the first time I've ever felt like living is decay in slow motion. This might be my first panic attack. I know I'm drawing more attention to *me* than the question itself. Emily rolls her eyes and turns away to eat her lunch.

Xenophobia doesn't always look like a monument of shame. It doesn't always look like ridicule and jeering. It looks like a room full of people and nobody to sit with. It looks like conversations buzzing all around me with no way in. It looks like one person at a time, taking notice of the ways in which I differ, and expressing quiet disinterest and revulsion. No one, big public humiliation. Many small, private disappointments.

Years later, my mother and I will call these *rice balls* around white people. It's a functional name at best. I can't help but feel that in the process of translating and explaining, some element of poetry evaporates from the name.

It could be any day of the week, it could coincide with a birthday or a holiday, it doesn't matter. Where it falls is random. Maybe there's a sale on pork or my father's run especially ragged at work, maybe my mother is bored. Whatever the case, if I stop by the family home at the right time, there it will be. The process unfolding with no big whoop about it, happening like this could be any other day, any other meal.

My mother cleaves the bones loose from a huge hunk of pork belly. She fills a sauté pan with green tea powder, star anise, quartered onions, slivers of ginger, and twelve cloves of garlic. She halves the length of pork belly and folds the chunks into the pan skin-side up like two fat snakes of raw dough.

I like to take a seat in the kitchen and watch the glass lid sweat while she prepares a slaw of red pepper paste, slivers of radish, and glistening raw oysters. A pot of five-grain rice steams away in a pressure cooker on the countertop, next to a stack of fresh napa cabbage leaves awaiting a quick pickling, all white and mute yellow like young daisies.

This is called 쌈. Or at least a variation of it. 쌈 can mean anything. The word essentially means *wrapped*. We eat variations like bite-sized pieces of grilled beef tenderloin dipped in a mixture of sesame seed oil, salt, and pepper, wrapped in lettuce with raw garlic and soy paste. Or grilled pork stained crimson with a spiced marinade. Sometimes we eat cold slices of raw fish wrapped in perilla leaves, with a sweet red chili dipping sauce.

It must be less disorienting for my husband to hear me speak full Korean on the phone than it is to be seated at dinner with me and my parents. My mother always tries to make something special that he's never eaten before. Tonight, we're having 보쌈. She shows him how it's eaten in the best English she can muster, interjecting several Korean expressions of uncertainty.

'You eat it like this,' she says. She picks up a piece of pork belly and pats it against a bed of rice inside her cabbage leaf. Her chopsticks are quick, deliberate. 'Next the oyster salad.' My mother gives the ending Ds of words like *salad* syllables of their own. 'Oh, is very delicious. Is like, 거 뭐야? Like special treat, for you. My new son.'

My father makes some joke about never expecting a son-in-law at this table. I turn to him and say, '아니 왜 그려서? That's so not necessary.' The deadpan American English snark I've picked up from living here in conjunction with a melodramatic child's *why are you like this*, slurred by a rural Korean dialect that my grandmother taught me. It's a dialect a lot of metropolitan Koreans can't even understand.

Bryan eats timidly beneath my father's close gaze, flexing his chopsticks as everyone marvels at how well he does for a white boy. My father chides him endlessly on how little rice he eats. 'Isn't it so salty,' my parents want to know. 'You must take more rice,' my father will say. 'Americans are so skinny.' But Bryan didn't grow up how we did, he grew up in a nice Midwestern home where his mother never stuffed a whole pork wrap the size of her fist in her mouth, chewing for the next five minutes while assembling a new one. His restraint is actually a little offensive to us in some way. It's inconceivable to us that someone would eat all these fermented, seasoned, marinated dishes with no rice to temper the sourness and salt. He doesn't understand how our food is really supposed to taste, and it feels like he's telling us he doesn't care.

But Bryan just wants to try everything. A little bit of everything without getting too full on a boring old side of rice. It's all so new for him.

Rice is present at every single meal in a Korean household. In fact, our word for *food* or *meal*—밥—also specifically means rice. Rice is a must-have and to call it a *side* is somehow too simplified. It's more like 반찬, ranging from as pedestrian as kimchi or tofu, to as lavish as spicy grilled octopus and sirloin, are the sides. He's got it backwards.

Rice doesn't even need a sidekick. There's fried rice made with kimchi or sweet ground beef and onions. There's the cold dish 비빔밥, meaning *mixed rice*, made with dressed vegetables, pepper paste, and a runny fried egg on top, or 회덮밥 with raw fish and peppers, garlic, a garland of mugwort. For a snack we eat 떡, rice flour kneaded into chewy dough.

One could say rice is almost as important as water. Yet like the taste of water, my deep reverence for rice is ineffable. I understand why Bryan doesn't get it. I can explain and explain the cultural significance of rice until he concedes its importance, but he'll never be more than a tourist. He'll never be more than a voyeur, an audience. He wasn't there when my mother stirred rice flour and water into glue to affix old photographs to the pages of a scrapbook. He wasn't there when she showed me how it's done and proclaimed what wonders live inside a single grain of rice. He wasn't there when she mixed that same slurry into chili paste for kimchi or tamed peeling wallpaper with it. He wasn't there when she used it to fix a punctured paper screen. Rice taught me imagination. Rice taught me wonder and nostalgia. But he wasn't there.

A white friend of Bryan's buys herself a fermenting crock for Christmas. She says she wants to try her hand at making kimchi. As if it's something to *try one's hand at*. I have never heard of such a thing as a fermenting crock.

Her kimchi comes out soggy and wilted, the leaves translucent yellow like snot, shredding from nothing but the weight of their own dampness. I can't explain to her exactly what went wrong, but just by looking I can tell it's very wrong.

When I was a toddler, I was already peeling whole onions and cloves of garlic. I've been doing that shit so long, I can probably do it with one hand and my eyes closed. I'd sit next to a big metal basin with my great-grandmother, shucking dozens of these things smooth. My grandmother and my mother would sit at a different basin, one mixing rice flour and water into gruel, the other rubbing coarse-ground salt into halved heads of napa cabbage. They'd make at least six heads at a time. Otherwise, all the hours of effort and mess weren't worth it.

They'd tuck salt along the veins of the leaves on each head. The cabbage had to sit for at least two hours, drinking up the moisture and salt. While waiting, somebody would sliver up matchsticks of radish and carrot. Chop up garlic chives and water dropwort, mince some ginger, salted shrimp paste, an onion, and thirty cloves of garlic to mix with several cups of red pepper powder into a rice slurry. This was rubbed into all six heads of napa cabbage, between every single leaf, with bare hands.

You hear these stories about beauty rituals, girls learning to groom themselves. We had none of that. What we did in the bathroom or in front of a mirror was our business to figure out. The women of my mother's family did not shave or wax their legs. Preparing kimchi was the rite of passage in our house. This was the good pain our mothers taught us. The sting of salt. The kind of pain that made us tough and numb. The kind of pain that by looking, one would never think a shriveled, paper-skinned, shrimp-spined woman like my grandmother would withstand for hours at a time.

My mother is a woman who sleeps with curlers in her hair. I don't know why or how to use those curlers. My mother is a woman who makes kimchi. I know why and how to make kimchi.

Part of me feels vindicated when that white girl's batch of kimchi comes out all wrong. When she asks what she did wrong, I don't know where to start.

So there I am sitting in front of the TV when my husband, a pink-collar white boy out of rural Illinois with the long diphthongs to prove it, sets a plate of something in front of me. He's tried his hand at an omelet with leftover pork belly, kimchi, hoisin, a little bit of pepper paste, throwing all that Far East goodness I keep around into some kind of an experiment. Here's the thing—it's *delicious*. Bryan slings some of the best burgers and skirt steak sandwiches I've ever had. He makes his living at this bar and grill in downtown Palatine, a bluesy rock-n-roll joint where he's the chef, and it's hard to dismiss his comfort noshes as simple *bar food* when he's roasting marrow in the oven for his chili. When he's making his own sundried tomato gravy for the meatloaf. He knows his shit.

But I'm struck by a wave of defensiveness. Even though it's a good, hot plate of food, I feel offended. There's just something about it. Like if I were to pick it apart, I could say he didn't caramelize the kimchi, which any Korean worth their salt knows to do. But I try to remind myself this is my husband making me breakfast. We're not on an episode of *Chopped*.

It's like any time a white friend suggests Korean barbeque. Or when I see a Food Network special where some tattooed white dude with a nineteenth-century-looking beard-and-mustache combo introduces viewers to this kimchi al pastor bánh mì monstrosity he peddles from a food truck that sends out location tweets. It's like when white people tell me how much they love *kim-chee* and *bull-go-ghee*, and the words just roll off their tongues as if there exists nothing irreconcilable between the two languages.

It's like, *don't touch my shit*.

It's difficult to articulate because I know it's not rational. But as a bilingual immigrant from Korea, as someone who code-switches between Korean and English daily while running errands or going to the supermarket, not to mention the second-nature combination of the languages that I'll speak with my parents and siblings, switching on and switching off these at times unfeasibly different sounds, dialects, grammatical structures? It's fucking irritating. I don't want to be stingy about who gets to enjoy all those fermented wonders—I'm glad the stigma around our stinky wares is dissolving away. But when my husband brings me a plate of food he made out of guesswork with a list of ingredients I've curated over the years of my burgeoning adulthood with the implicit help of my mother, my grandmother, and my grandmother's mother who taught me the patience of peeling dozens of garlic cloves in a sitting with bare hands, it puts me in *snap-me-off-a-hickory-switch* mode.

It surprises me when I meet someone so interested in Korean food that they go so far as to make their own kimchi at home, who then goes on to confess they've never met a Korean person before. There's a part of me that wishes they'd ask me what I think, how I feel, instead of insisting how friendly they are. Instead of Bryan chucking a bunch of Asian ingredients together, I wish he'd ask me how something is made. When I bring home a bowl of 설렁탕, I kind of wish he'd taste it, appreciate it, ask me how it's made, ask me when I used to eat this as a child, what does it mean to our people, before he goes digging around for the sriracha.

Here's what I'd tell him or any white friend if they'd ask first.

Get the sriracha away from your 설렁탕 or so help me. That's a personal insult to my grandmother *and* the country of Thailand at large.

This dish is not meant to be spicy. Though the ethnocentric landscape of the Western cultural lexicon may have led you to believe everything Korean is spicy, this is something else. We are more than one palate of flavors. There is a time and place for things.

설렁탕, to me, is a dish that saved my life. When a doctor said I was too skinny as a baby, my grandmother rinsed the leg bones of an ox and simmered them for hours and hours, nestled into a pot with a whole onion, a pound and a half of radish. Meat sloughed from bone, soft as cream. Marrow melted into a rich broth that held the complexion of milk. It isn't possible to make less than a week's worth of 설렁탕—it takes too much work to throw away on one meal, and the broth can't be squeezed out with less than two heaping pounds of bones. My grandmother condensed this bobbing protein, all this fatty warmth, into a bottle of formula just for me. She thought it would help me put on weight. And it did. She'd serve whatever was left of the soup to the family as dinner for weeks on end. She would float chopped green onions and silvery hanks of vermicelli in a bowl of 설렁탕, and set a table with a bowl of rice for each of my parents, her husband, herself. Those bones are throw-away cuts here—some butchers give that shit away. But for my family, ox bones were precious. 설렁탕 is a delicacy. A luxury to keep you warm through winter.

We keep a shallow dish of salt and pepper at the center of the table to season our own bowls. It's not meant to be spicy. The marrow should be enough to warm you, if you pay attention and let it. The painstaking preparation enough to stay your hand. Or so help me.

When I set a dish in front of someone, when I take somebody by the hand and walk them through the plaza of a Korean supermarket or restaurant or my mother's kitchen, I'm not there to feed them something new. Our recipes are not party tricks. I'm trying to share something rich, and old, and long-simmered. Something beyond the names for things. Something about comfort and tenderness, something familiar, save for perhaps in another language.

My mother thinks I'm getting dangerously fat. She suggests a multitude of diets and cosmetic surgeries we can't afford. 'Stop eating like such a pig,' she says. She says that word a lot, *pig*. She keeps the kitchen on lockdown and shoos me away if she catches me nearby. She watches the fridge like a hawk, keeping careful inventory of fatty foods. She puts me on diet pills, stuffs me into undersized, sweat-stained clothes, and makes me run laps at school after hours in front of everyone. She tells me I can pick out nicer clothes when my body earns them.

Anywhere my mother pushes, I pull at the other end. She monitors the fridge, I hoard junk food under my bed. I'm either holed up in my room with the door shut or I'm out with friends. I talk less. I cloister more. She bursts into my room in the middle of the night, interrupting what little sleep I am getting to perform tongue-prayer blessings. She roots through my things and calls it cleaning. She says, 'You live like such a pig.' She searches my pockets and bags every day and demands to know what I tell people about her.

My friends all agree that my mom is weird and fucked up and crazy. I try to laugh it off until they start offering me a place to stay.

The only volumes in our house are YELLING and ICY SILENCE. I have feverish nightmares and barely sleep. I'm realizing being beaten isn't normal, or at least isn't healthy. I'm realizing I rarely see my father. When I do, he always wants a hug but he never asks how I am. My mother has no concept of boundaries. I'm nothing but an extension of her brutal self-loathing. Even though I haven't learned the right words for that concept yet, my body knows. My fat body is her fat body. My wide nose is her wide nose. My monolids are hers. My knock knees are hers. My trauma-fixed gaze is hers. I'm angry and tense all the time. My body seethes and boils and pushes outward. It's reaching for someplace peaceful and big enough.

I'm fourteen years old. I keep a notebook full of scribbles and violent doodles pressed nearly through the paper. I write letters to my mother in here. This notebook is the only thing I own. It's where I keep my meanest, saddest thoughts so I don't have to say them out loud.

One day my mother is sitting by the door when I get home from school. She shakes the notebook in my face, her hair wild and her knuckles white with rage. 'What is this!' she demands. She reads passages aloud to me, twisting and shredding the pages in anger. *If I'm such a pig, why don't you cut me open and eat me?* She says, 'This is disgusting.' She says, 'How can you think like this.' She says, 'What's wrong with you. Why are you so angry.'

I don't know how to explain when the answers are in her hands. I don't show her because she doesn't want to see.

There's this old anti-drug PSA where a father confronts his son about his habit. He asks, 'Who taught you how to do this stuff?' and the kid says, 'I learned it from watching you.' It's kind of like that. Kind of.

I learn to give up on the notion of being my own anything but there's nothing revelatory about the lesson. All it means is that now there's nowhere for my mean, sad thoughts to go. It only further entrenches the same patterns: I push, she pulls. I binge and purge. I break things. I cry. I cut myself. I pull away, she pushes in. She strips the locks off bathroom doors. I beg for help. She hosts prayer meetings. I swallow everything. She testifies my secrets to the whole congregation.

I'm downing my father's scotch, alone, fourteen years old, while she's already writing the story of my salvation. The story of her sacrifice for the pulpit.

THE GOLDFISH AND THE EEL

IN A DREAM, MY MOTHER BUYS A GOLDFISH at a kiosk with blue vinyl awnings that remind me of where I was born: open markets in South Korea where old women slung skewered fishcake and silkworms from steaming broth, where men with leathery faces and fingerless gloves came hauling charcoal grills each winter to sell fresh-roasted chestnuts in paper bags.

The goldfish my mother buys outgrows its bowl, then another, then a third. I frantically rummage the house looking for anything big enough to contain the fish and it ends up in our bathtub.

I fill the tub with water, but while my back is turned, the fish absorbs it like a sponge. I turn the faucet and again the water vanishes as soon as I catch my breath. This enormous fish lies on its side, eyes silvery and gaping like the bowl of a spoon, flapping its lips, shaking the tiles of our bathroom with each thrash of its body. It's as desperate for air as I am to save it. I'm filling and filling the tub. The task feels endless, doomed. There's no room to bathe.

When I wake up, my body is lead. Sinking.

My mother birthed me in a Seoul hospital in 1990. Her hips were too narrow for natural birth. She lay back in stirrups pushing and sobbing as they sucked me out with tubes and motors. She didn't even want me. She didn't really know what she wanted. Nobody asked. Imagine being a woman in 1990. Imagine being a Korean woman in 1990. But there she was. Naked and numb from the waist down like her entire sexual history as far as I can guess. Suddenly holding me.

Safety and innocence don't exist in nature. Childhood is a social construct, an ideological fever dream afforded those whose mothers call miracles rather than eye from an ambivalent distance, fists clenched in hopes that we don't cry, for god's sake, again.

I don't think about my childhood much. I forget pieces all the time. I'm great at forgetting, which is not a useful skill as a writer. But if I shut my eyes tight, here's what I see: my mother flying into a rage; my father shrinking through our doorway on another business trip with the promise of a souvenir but no date of return; cowering, always cowering; Disney World one year, scabby bedbug bites and growling stomachs the next; selling plasma at a clinic with my mom at six years old and eyeing the cookie they've promised while my blood flows through a tube; toppling over as an infant, formula dripping down my face because no one is supporting the bottle but me; waking up to an empty house, aching someplace mysterious like the gut but not quite; my mother's growing irritation as she asks *are you hungry, are you sick* and I tell her I don't know, I don't know, it just aches, dull, like something's missing but I'm heavy and maybe floating or shrinking or vanishing all at once, like a slow wither.

I'm sitting in a crowded classroom one day twenty years later when suddenly I feel that ache again and this time I know its name is loneliness.

I remember my mother clenching her fists as I rattle on about this feeling, another problem she can't solve. Once her diagnostic questions stop, I ask when my dad's coming home.

The answer always begins with *maybe*. Sometimes it ends with a backhand.

There's this story my mother keeps in her back pocket for when it gets too quiet, a story she turns to at parties for shock or entertainment value. I don't understand why it's still up there with so many birthdays and firsts and spankings forgotten, but regardless, I can't shake it.

My mother grew up in a village where she'd duck in and out of clear flowing streams for fun in the springtime. The way she tells it, she's the sort of girl who plucks flowers and presses them in journals. She watches dragonflies, lizards, fish. Sometimes she catches them in a jar. One day she scoops a skinny little eel and one of those goldfish with the big bulgy eyes into a glass jar and carries them home.

My mother feeds them flake food from a pet store. She gives each one a name. They get along well. She comes home from school each day, takes off her shoes, and watches them while doing homework at her desk by the sunny windowsill. Then she forgets to feed them for a week straight.

The goldfish floats around listlessly bumping into the glass walls of the jar. My mother stares at the empty sockets where there once shined big bulgy eyes. The skinny little eel got so hungry that it ate its companion's eyeballs. Just the eyeballs.

This story bounces around my skull for all my first years and after that initial *pow*, the ricochet of childhood, the memory slows its momentum. It idles leisurely around in this meandering path guided by nothing but the shimmering chaos of how things plain happen until one day I'm standing in the shower thinking about all the worst things I've ever done.

I got an anger problem. A drug problem. A sex problem. An intimacy problem. I got anxiety. Bipolar disorder. I got a problem with disordered attachment and if you kiss me I might blow up your phone for two days to make sure you're not out to hurt me or use me or that you really do like me, just to make sure you know I'm a human being and not a toy, make sure I didn't hurt you in some mystical time-release way or that you don't secretly find my body repulsive or I don't know. I don't know.

My brain shorts out while no one is home. I throw Bryan's guitars around the room, trash the kitchen, break the birthday gift I bought him. It's one of the worst things I've ever done and I've done it more than once. More than twice.

I'm sorry. I know I'm not a good person.

I'm sorry. But I don't believe in bad people either.

Raising me is on my mother's list of the worst things she's ever done—thinking about it sends her into a frenzy of prayer and my father to sleep on the couch. She finds Jesus. I find drugs and sex and speeding down the interstate. I find bad boyfriends and hospital debts. I find bigger reasons to hurt than all the things my parents ever did or didn't do. I'm not actually great at forgetting anything. I'm great at repressing and white-knuckling like nothing's wrong or at least that what's wrong is some nebulous secret that serves no purpose in being unfolded. Even writing this, I find myself losing my place or suddenly the thought vanishing from my head because it's easier to leave everything behind than carry it with you when you're always running. But running is futile. Being beaten and shaken, forced to pack a bag of toys and abandoned in a crowded open market full of old women slinging skewered fishcakes under blue vinyl awnings, that shit leaves marks on you and not just the kind that purple, yellow, and fade. It leaves you on the other end of screaming diatribes from your boyfriend over the phone and calling him back when you think he's sober. It leaves you chasing people you don't love because they love you even less. It leaves you *knowing* people who love you can do horrendous, inexcusably fucked up shit to you.

As much as love is this miraculous practice of caring for and regarding someone in a certain dazzling light, I know it's not enough on its own. Because as much as my mom and I both know she failed to love me right, we also both know she always did love me. That's why love can be both arbitrary and dangerous.

Depressive episodes hit like boiling water, like I fuck off to the bathroom for a bit while a pot's simmering and the moment I get back it's rolling out onto the stove. Like so many things it begins and ends with forgetting: I forget to text back, I forget to clip my nails, I forget to eat, I forget, period.

So it takes six hours today, but I get out of bed and into the shower. This dread washes over me. I have to wash and feed this body every day until the day I die. I have to clip these nails every week until the day I die. I have to pay the phone bill every month until the day I die. It feels endlessly tedious. I'm stuck standing under the water. Skin pruning. Forgetting how to move because I've forgotten where I need to go and I'm thinking about that fucking eel and goldfish again because it always seems to come up when I'm like this.

I can hear my mom's coy laugh as she tells this story, thick meaty fingers looped through the handle of a teacup while church friends listen and nibble biscuits. The story never reaches any natural conclusion. It's this macabre scene, a fish missing its eyes in a sunlit jar. That's it. She says, 'That's what happens when you don't feed fish, I guess.' So glib. I wonder how you can forget something a foot from your bed for a single day, let alone a week straight. Then I remember my grandma's failing kidneys and fainting spells, her frail bird bones. She's suffered from some atypical variety of lupus for as long as my mother can remember. I picture my mother kicking off her shoes, sliding across the floor to her mother's bed to make sure nobody's died. I picture her dozing off with her chin on her mother's lap as the eel grows hungrier. My grandfather loosening his tie as he walks in from work, dreading the sight of his wife withering away in bed, tripping over shoes all scattered about in haste, seeing scuff marks on the floor, ripping my mother away from her mother's bed to slap her legs raw and red with a hickory switch from the backyard.

These things happen.

Still wet from the shower, I start setting up this internet modem I bought to shave ten bucks off the Comcast bill. Turns out my laptop doesn't have an Ethernet port and Bryan's laptop is dead and missing its charger. I can't help but think of the time Pauly called up Comcast over some billing issue, cussed out the customer service dude, hung up, and threw his cell phone at me while screaming. It's a quick flash that only further infuriates me as I root around our apartment for the charger. I'm texting Bryan over and over while he's at work. It's escalating, my body pulses with anger and fear and blood, I say I hate him, I say I hate living with him, I say worse and worse things, more and more dishonest things just to be hurtful even though I know he's not ignoring me on purpose. My dog Leroy cowers under a desk as I trash the apartment and the only honest thing I text my husband in that moment is *i want to fucking kill myself.*

I'm rocking back and forth on the couch. I just need to set up this modem. That will fix everything. It'll fix me.

Bryan finally replies while he's on break, *Baby, you should take a Xanax. I'm sorry I can't be there. I love you. Please be okay.*

Leroy watches me from across the room, this anxious little poodle mix with eyes as cavernous as space, as black as mine. She doesn't look away. She's more afraid for me than of me.

I call my father while he's at church and tell him I'm having a massive panic attack but it's fine, everything's fine, can you please bring over your laptop because I kind of feel like I might die a little bit. I hear my mom in the background, a frantic spur of questions in Korean.

My father says he's leaving right now. I put the phone down and take a half milligram of Xanax. I sit back down. Leroy slinks over from under the desk while I cry and cry and say, 'I'm sorry, I'm so sorry.' She nuzzles my wrist, digging her claws into my thigh like she wants to make sure I'm still here.

When my dad arrives, he offers to hook up the internet for me at first but sees that I need this ritual. I need to do this one thing right today. He says, 'Don't worry about it,' through his thick Korean accent and a grimace. He manages some quiet laughter and watches me thread a cable from a blinking modem to his laptop while I sit on the floor in a calm daze. The Xanax slurs my words but steadies my hand and my dad says he can tell I took something. He doesn't pass judgment. He only observes.

Is this what he did for my mother?

Those nights he came home to a bruised child and a trembling wife, is this what he did? As I lay crying in a dark room with hand-shaped welts stinging my back, was he silently watching with a hand on my mother's back, saying *don't worry* through a grimace?

His eyes are steady and soft. He asks when Bryan will be home. He says my mom's been missing me since I moved out. She's bringing food over later. I must be going without a lot of home-cooked Korean.

He doesn't scan the room. He doesn't point out the toppled furniture.

He says, 'It's okay.'

He says, 'I'm sorry it took so long.'

HERE'S SOMETHING ELSE I'VE NEVER TOLD ANYONE.

I'm ten years old and all my hair is falling out. The truth is I've been pulling it out but it feels strange to say I'm doing it because if anything it feels like the doing is taking hold of me. It started when I was three years old and I swear it was just after the neighbor boy molested me but I don't want to talk about that very much. Only that everyone seemed angry with me so I felt ashamed and being honest began to feel dangerous but the point is that's when it started. It's called trichotillomania if someone must quench a sick curiosity to Google it but the point is everyone keeps seeming angry with me so I keep feeling ashamed. I'm growing bald spots. My mother takes me to a doctor and I never look him in the eye even once. He keeps asking are you sure you're not doing this to yourself and I shake my head no because it doesn't feel like I'm doing anything but rather everything is happening to me. I don't have words for that yet. He has other patients to see and my mother says of course she's not doing it to herself my daughter isn't crazy. He sighs. He prescribes a topical ointment but warns my mother, it won't make any difference if she's doing this to herself. On the drive home my mother says there's something definitely wrong with me. She says there are so many demons in our family, so many demons inside of me and on my back.

I'm fourteen years old and I need a doctor.

I need a doctor. I need somebody, something, help. Every night I dream of car crashes and rape. Every dream is another dead end of my body's helpless wandering. There is nothing left to imagine so it tells nothing but the same painful truths. I need help. I need help I'm thinking of slitting my wrists I need somebody to help. The praying gets louder and more frequent but it stays the same amount of useless. Please I need a doctor. Help me I'm so sad. Help me I'm so alone. The nightmares only stop when I stop trying to sleep. Help me I feel hopeless and empty, something's so so wrong. Every time I tell the truth all I get is more of it. Help me Mom. Help me Dad. I need a doctor. The praying gets louder but the sadness stays the same.

Help I need somebody. I'd feel forsaken by God if I had ever felt kept. How I wish I could still believe in Him. Please I need a doctor, help.

Help me.

Help I'm hearing voices. I'm seeing things. I need a doctor.

I need a doctor.

My mother thinks the problem is demons, that all I need is a healthy exorcism and weekly bible study. My father disagrees but he can't seem to articulate why and isn't interested in fighting over it. He just says at least send the kid to the doctor and leaves the rest to his wife. He goes to work. He comes home. He goes to work. He doesn't come home.

My father learned to drink and hide. I'm learning all kinds of things.

The doctor asks what I've been experiencing and I rattle off a grocery list of symptoms. He seems skeptical but he writes dutifully in his legal pad. Auditory hallucinations. Thought blocks. Paranoid delusions.

Just as dutifully I am scouring the internet for every symptom that might be serious enough to warrant attention. Extreme mood swings. Feelings of hopelessness and suicidal ideation. Racing thoughts. Some of these aren't true but I don't know how to backtrack. I don't want to go back to feeling helpless and alone. Even when he prescribes anti-psychotics I say nothing, only thank you. I'm just grateful to be seen. I let the medications slow me down. I let my notebooks sit untouched for months.

I'm not writing because I'm not thinking. I'm not thinking because I'm not feeling. People will tell me what I'm like years later because I won't remember.

SOME
NOTES ON HEALING

fistula \\'fis(h)-chə-lə\\
  1. *n.* an abnormal connection between organs.

  a. The piercer clamps my tongue with forceps and says *oh, that thing's just begging to be pierced*. This discomfort is layered and hard to describe. His rubber gloves are smooth like skin, I think, should be.

  The piercer hands me a pamphlet detailing aftercare instructions and winks.[1]

---

[1] An excerpt from *Beginner's Guide to Body Piercings*: 'Once the skin is pierced and jewelry is inserted, the body's immune system will react to the foreign object (i.e., a trusty 14-gauge implant grade titanium captive bead ring). Following this initial procedure, signs of inflammation such as swelling, redness, heat, or secretion of fluids are all normal and expected. During the healing process, the body produces new epithelial cells and tiny blood vessels around the puncture, forming a tunnel of tissue to accommodate jewelry. This network of flesh and blood flow is called fistula.'

2. *n.* a passage created surgically that leads from an organ to the body's surface to permit exchange of fluids or secretions. From Latin, meaning *pipe* or *flute*.

a. I'm on my period and half a bottle of Xanax when Dave comes over. I tell him not to, but he insists. I tell him not to at least three times and I'm crying on the phone when he knocks at my door. It's raining and I want to be alone. I want to feel close to someone without being touched. Does that make sense. Be seen without being looked at. Does that make sense. I want to be alone but not *feel* alone. Does that make sense. He says he's my friend. This is a secret code. It's raining and he's getting soaked out there. This is also code. I'm on my period and that's mostly all I remember. I say I'm on my period and he says then he won't need a condom. I'm on my back. I'm so tired. I'm on half a bottle of Xanax and Dave has been begging for me to give some up for an hour and three years. He's heavy like a storm. 'Do you feel how wet you are,' he says as he sheathes himself in blood. I'm already forgetting how it started but I know it's wrong.

b. The next time a man touches me, I reach for a knife I don't own.[2]

splinter \'splin(t)ər\
1. *v.* break or cause to break into small sharp fragments; separate into smaller units, typically as a result of disagreement.

---

[2] See: *fester.*

a. When I first meet Bryan, I notice he repeats words after a few beers. Especially after a few beers and a few rails of coke. It's perhaps compulsive. He'll say, 'I'm breathing, I'm breathing.' He'll say, 'I can't stop repeating, repeating,' while rocking back and forth, bug-eyed and confused like his body and will are barreling down separate paths, caught in a loop of awkward momentum. It reminds me of my mother mid-prayer. I fear the problem may be neurological.[3] My fear is perhaps compulsive.

b. My dealer Ronnie says she survived a ruptured spleen from a car crash decades ago, but this isn't the story. Despite X-rays upon X-rays, the doctors missed a shard of glass buried in her elbow. So her muscles stretched and folded over as she healed, wrapping this piece of windshield like a gift until the next time she gets X-rays taken and there it is. It takes a while to remember where she picked up this little souvenir. She says she carried this

[3] There was an unusual case of hydrocephalus in the news some years back. A French civil servant visits his doctor and CT scans reveal a shocking absence of gray matter, condensed and consumed by excess fluid and the resulting cranial pressure. His brains hug the walls of his skull as if shrinking from a cold touch. He is forty-four years old, of average intelligence or slightly below. An unnamed father of two. Doctors are baffled at first by his level of functioning, later crediting the phenomenon known as *plasticity*. The way a deaf person might gradually develop heightened perception in other senses of the body, the way a lazy eye is caught up to speed with a dark patch over its twin, this unnamed patient continued to speak, drive a car, and perform a civil service job on half a brain, frontal lobe learning how to gauge distance, cerebellum learning to count change at the supermarket. I wish I could ask those doctors what became of him and his family, about the potential outcomes of missing half your brain, of falling in love and building a life with someone who is missing half their brain.

piece of glass through her first abortion, first overdose, first and vehemently last marriage. The X-rays show multiple hairline fractures where her boyfriend's steel-toed boots made impact, but this is not the story.[4] Her body has learned its way around this piece of glass the way her tongue has learned its way around the word *no* as in *trust no man*.[5]

c. Sometimes during sex, Bryan looks at me like he wonders if something terrible has happened. I can't answer when he asks. My body breaks into parts with no binding awareness. Or each part of me has its own. An arm, a leg, a breast, each feeling and being felt.[6] This is the pain of my body remembering itself.[7] Like he asks if I'm okay and I say I don't know, I don't know, I don't know.

clavicle \'klavək(ə)l\

1. *n.* a bone of the vertebrate pectoral girdle typically serving to link the scapula and sternum—also called *collarbone*. From Latin *clavicula* meaning *small key*.

a. My mother picks the lock off my diary. She tells everyone *this child needs Jesus*. My mother searches my pockets and bag each time I walk in the house. She says *this child needs Jesus*. My mother finds a joint in my dresser drawer, but not the painkillers. She grabs my wrist so hard it purples and stripes. I snatch it back so hard something in her breaks. She cries *this child needs Jesus*. She gets on

---

[4] I'll be sober next year, though I don't know that yet.

[5] See: *hypervigilance*.

[6] See: *broken circuit*. See: *a dammed river*. See: *too many seams*.

[7] See: *trauma*.

her knees and claps her hands across my forehead to pray, leaning into a frenzied gibberish, speaking what she calls the blessed tongue.[8]

b. Summer, 1986: My mother is riding the bus home in Seoul as blinding white petals rain down from trees bricked off into grids, the weight of uncertainty slung low in her chest. Every day she leaves work pondering the purpose of a typist, the purpose of her college degree, the purpose of a woman in 1986, the future looming without promise, formless like dusk. She is suspended between graduation and husbandry, between ambition and tradition. My grandfather is arranging meetings with potential suitors. She is promised a husband in the next five years. She will undergo several cosmetic procedures in preparation for courtship and marriage—creases nipped along the eyelids as per Western traditions

---

[8]   Christianity thrived in Korea as a form of nationalistic resistance during Japan's annexation (1910–1945). Churches founded by Western missionaries proved a rare refuge for native Koreans in the face of Japan's assimilation efforts—stringent bans against the Korean language, enforcing Shinto practices and worship of the Japanese Emperor as deity. This fostered an ironic connection between the preservation of Korean culture and a Western religion.

Following liberation from Japanese rule and the separation of two Koreas, Christians fled from North Korea to South in search of religious freedom against a rising tide of Soviet influence. This marked a pronounced shift in population—an influx of Christians in the South, a former stronghold of churches left abandoned in the North—as well as a shift of meaning: Western religion repurposed as essentially Korean, Korean nationalism translated into anti-communism.

This history wedges itself as the fracture between my mother's love and my understanding of it.

of beauty, sparse eyebrows typical of Koreans tattooed darker.

My mother sits stiffly on a blue vinyl seat as the bus trundles through an intersection. She hears the lonely skid of tires against pavement. It happens quickly. She grips a hanging strap overhead as everything lurches forward. She is suspended in the force of a collision. She is collateral damage in the act of inertia. The bus rail snaps in half. Her clavicle snaps in half, a compound fracture to the music of careening steel. She will tell this story over and over to herself. The pain is not what she remembers later. There are people dying with names she'll never learn. The snap of bone sings a rush of possibility, this feeling she names Lord and Savior. She will tell this story over and over. She will tell this story over and over to the pastor, who feels like Father, God in Heaven. She is compounded risk in the palm of Christ, in the arms of a congregation. She tells this story over and over. She is suspended in the ecstasy of conversion.[9]

c. Summer, 1986: My father is boarding a subway train miles away in a different district of the city. His shirts and ties are wrinkled. He eats more instant noodles than his yearly salary would suggest. His coworkers chide him for being single, for living without a wife to keep him sharp.

---

[9] To this day, my mother will press her meaty fingers into the dip of her collarbone, feeling its crookedness in times of hardship and waning faith. To this day, my mother says she is waiting for me to have a car crash of my own.

d. Summer, 2014: My mother says she never wanted children and when I ask what it is she did want, she trails off into the story of her bus accident again. I am twenty-four years old when I realize consent was never etched into her vocabulary.

splinter \\'splin(t)ər\\
    2. *n.* a small needlelike particle, especially embedded in the skin.

    a. I inspect Bryan's hand under the light. I prod a dark speck buried in that first layer of thick, whorled skin on his thumb.[10] Sharp pain. The smell of iodine. Relief like cold water.[11] He winces, but doesn't jerk away.[12] It's strange how the body acts. And reacts. Strange how without intervention, the threat of a splinter swells up his body's defenses, swells up the skin with fluid and pressure, all in the name of pushing out the offending object days later.[13] How the feel of Bryan's hands grazing my legs makes me feel softer as though I didn't know the softness of my body until his touch hissed along my skin.

    Strange how the body reacts. Strange how excision risks infection. Strange how without intervention, the affected area will continue to ache vaguely.

---

[10] Skin so tough it caught a splinter that went unnoticed until squeezed. Skin so tough it aches now, pinched open to the air with tweezers. Translucent and milky when bloated with water. Scabrous and warm like fresh-baked bread after roasting and grilling for hours at work.

[11] See: *shiver.*

[12] The same way I am learning the instinct of tenderness again.

[13] This process is called *rejection.*

nodule \\'näjo̅ol\\

1.   *n.* a small rounded lump of matter distinct from its surroundings.

a. Bryan refuses to take his shirt off in public. He balks at the thought of visiting the beach. Sometimes he even resists being looked at with the lights on.

The left side of his chest is flatter than the right. His left nipple is smaller, the surface almost concave. Just enough hollow for a shadow to pool in. He points this out when he's sad. He's tried everything. Every workout imaginable, as many reps as he can muster. The right side will bulk up, but not the left. There's just nothing there. He says something is missing. It was always missing.[14]

He points this out when I'm sad. He will watch me searching the mirror for things I didn't know to hate. He will tap that shallow dip of his chest because he knows the feeling of not being enough of something.

b. The dentist taps my right mandibular second molar. She says, 'It's huge.' Her assistant laughs softly. 'Well, look at that.' It's approximately three millimeters wider than its twin on my left, two millimeters taller. I ask how unusual it is. She tells me it's no cause for concern, medically speaking. That's not what I'm asking.

I compare my right breast against my left. They seem identical. My right hand against my left. They seem iden-

---

[14] The *pectoralis major*, or something. Maybe his mother was a smoker, maybe she liked her cocktails, maybe the research wasn't out there yet, or something.

tical. This reassurance comes with unease.[15] The classification of a single tooth as anomaly weighs like bricks balanced atop a pin, one freak in a dentist's twenty years of experience.

What about my kidneys, what about my ovaries, my lungs, lymph nodes, ribs, what else, what else. I search my reflection for what else until I find it.

An uneven drape in my epicanthic folds, like someone has drawn the curtains without looking.

The crooked flare of a nostril.

An inch-long difference between my left ear and my right.

The faults come tumbling like I've flung the cabinets wide open with too much haste.

2. *n.* a swelling on the root of a plant. From Latin, meaning *little knot.*

a. The third time Bryan proposes, he is swaying side to side with his hands splayed across his grin and bulging eyes. He slurs, 'You should just marry me,' but I laugh it off because of all the cocaine and booze. I laugh it off because he suggests but doesn't ask.

---

[15] Julie Andrews was forced to quit the 1997 Broadway run of *Victor/Victoria* due to a hoarseness in her voice that was diagnosed as nodules (possibly cancerous), which she promptly had surgically removed. A decade later, she discovered that the nodules had never existed. The strain of the show had crimped her larynx. The strain of playing a woman playing a man, hurtling up and down her range caused what she now calls *striations.* Her voice never returned. There was a lawsuit. The doctor had removed what was never there, destroying what actually was. And so the smallest things can sometimes lead to the largest things, especially in a doctor's office.

I don't know it yet, but he's aching with disappointment. I don't know it yet, but he's afraid I'll say no and I'm afraid he's just drunk.

I won't let myself know it yet, but I want to say yes and there are reasons I can't seem to understand while we're both this fucked up.[16] When I laugh and say *are you fucking serious* he says *did you really think I was* and we snort another line but it gets a little quieter. He twitches and shivers, lying back on the bed with his eyes closed.

It feels as though we are skirting the precipice of something, as though the only edges of this memory are those of his body defining itself against mine because the rest hurts too much to keep, for reasons we don't know how to know yet.

I am reaching over to touch him, to find that boundary which makes my body real and makes the experience it occupies real, in the only way I understand.

I ask, 'Do you really love me?'

'Yes.'

'Why do you love me?'

'I don't know. I guess I just do.'

I curl up against him and the left side of his chest welcomes my cheek. Welcomes the curve of my face like hunger.

---

[16] These reasons will only seem wholly clear afterwards, revealing in a slow bloom as I drag myself to twelve-step meetings, support groups, to therapy, as I erase my rapist's number from my phone and get back in school, as I wake shaking from a nightmare and Bryan holds me, saying, 'I'm here,' 'I won't go,' and 'I promise.' Each time he says *I'm sorry* for things he didn't do to me.

i kind of have been mulling something over. i think a big reason why this last stretch of the book has been so hard is i don't feel like i'm necessarily "recovered" or even really "recovering." like i still have PTSD, i still have problems, i still double take when i'm out in public because i think i saw [redacted]. i'm still cagey and unfriendly to everyone. i feel like the natural conclusion is supposed to be reflective and that's what's expected of me and a book like this but i simply don't have anything like that to offer. i have a lot of new ~tools and coping skills~ i guess but i'm still kind of the same mentally ill fuck up from before i met him and while i was with him, the same fuck up who can't afford therapy or medication. in a lot of ways i'm still in the same place as i was at the end of the bedbug essay. the problems keep popping up and settling down and i'm just trying to keep it under control but sometimes its guaranteed that i'm going to spin out and i'm sort of just holding hands with bryan and staring down that trajectory and hoping feebly that i keep getting by y'know, and i have this very bad feeling like i'm letting Someone down because it's not the kind of story people want, it's kinda bleak and it goes in circles and doesn't go anywhere all that far? i feel like people want everybody to RECOVER and the story of long term coping doesn't look like any kind of valuable revelation

WHAT'S
THIS BITCH DOING

Sometimes you don't know what it is you need, but the need is sharp and constant. Blame it on your daddy issues. Your mommy issues. Bounce from one inappropriate liaison to the next. It's always needling you from inside your gut. You are crying all the time. You are writing a letter addressed to anyone. *I don't know what I'm looking for, but I'm so lonely*, you write in your ad. You're looking for a therapist in an inbox full of strange men.

One reply simply says: *maybe you need a good hot dicking.*

THE BEST I CAN DO

I tell the lonely men of Craigslist that I, too, am lonely. Hello, Strictly Platonic section of Craigslist. I am twenty-three years old. I have a drug problem but I'm dry right now. I have an eating disorder but it's whatever. I guess you could call me a sexual compulsive or something like that. I am trying not to act out but I am running out of phone numbers. I want to be your friend. I want to be your mom. I need you to be mine. I love you already. Tell me your story.

Amidst the fifty-some email responses I receive, one stands out in its stark, biting humor:

> *Last summer, the heat was crazy and traffic was at a total standstill on my way to work. So I rammed someone else's car at the tollbooth on I-90.*
>
> *I have great insurance.*

II. CROCODILE BIRD

The Egyptian plover (*Pluvianus aegyptius*) is the only member of the genus *Pluvianus*. A wader species with long, slim legs and striking plumage, it inhabits tropical sub-Saharan Africa and breeds on the sandbars of the Nile.

It is also known, erroneously, as the *crocodile bird*.

III. FAJITAS

Pauly looks nothing like he does in his photo.

In the photo, he's winding a baseball bat back. He's squinting in the heat, sand kicking up around him. He's lean, but his arms and neck are well-muscled. The sun washes away all his scars.

Looking at him in the parking lot of Marguerita's restaurant on Golf Road, shadowed against the peachy fake adobe walls, it's immediately apparent that the photo is at least a decade old. Pauly is skinny, like Fiona Apple in 'Criminal' skinny, but six feet tall and severely pockmarked. His eyes are wild. Something about him scares me. The way he lumbers and gestures, sneaky but menacing at once. It scares me. And he sees it.

'Sung. You're Sung, aren't you? It's me, Pauly. Did I scare you?'

There's hurt in his eyes. He never breaks eye contact but his gaze lacks any cool, easy sense of intimacy. Looking at him is like watching something jerk helplessly in the wind. He looks at me like he knows he looks nothing like his picture. Like he's hoping I stay to eat dinner but he's not expecting it. Like he's lonely and he likes me.

Looking at him, I don't feel self-conscious about my thinning hair or weight or nervous tics.

IV. TEETH

The crocodile has the most acidic stomach of any vertebrate. It can easily digest bones, hooves, and horns. A predator with a staggeringly slow metabolism, it can wait hours or even days for prey to draw near—making the ambush when the moment is ripe. A crocodile's diet varies greatly depending on size and age, but it consists mostly of fish, amphibians, reptiles, mammals, and birds. It occasionally cannibalizes smaller crocodiles.

The crocodile's jaws bite down with immense force, by far the strongest bite of any animal. Its teeth are ill-suited for tearing flesh, but rather excel at grabbing and holding on due to this ferocious strength. Sharper teeth, like those of a shark, would easily lop off the limbs of prey animals and offer an escape route. The crocodile's duller, sparser teeth allow it to engulf its prey in one piece.

This is how a crocodile feeds, by trapping its prey.

V. BOILING THE FROG

There's no point at which I feel tricked. I am not the unsuspecting frog in the water, heated so gradually that I boil to death. I have knowingly measured the stakes, inspected the stove, and decided that the prospect of grocery shopping for Pauly, cleaning his house, pouring his whiskey and waters, and letting him fuck me is a better way to live than whatever's out there. I have assessed my reflection in the mirror, combed over my sparse ratty hair, pressed blood from my acid-scorched gums, and decided confidently: *This is the best I can do.*

Even if his tirades leave me nervously fidgeting all day, worried that the cashier can tell something's wrong. Even if he makes snide remarks about my appearance and won't let me leave the house without a wig on. Even if he takes subtle digs at my friends and undermines our relationships, discouraging my love for anyone else. Even if he has this *friend* who sleeps over two nights a week, when I'm not allowed in his home.

He lies constantly, with complete ease. When I catch him in his lies, he laughs in my face. He also laughs when he sees blood on his fingers or cock. He says, 'Damn, baby. You better wash up.'

I tell myself I can take it.

All of this hurts and maybe even scares me. But none of it shocks me. This is a forty-six-year-old man I met on Craigslist. A Gulf War veteran with untreated PTSD. Binge drinker extraordinaire. Unrepentant racist and misogynist. I know all this. He doesn't even try to hide it. His abusive tirades, his toxic narcissism, his domineering tactics, are exactly what I would expect of a man like this.

Maybe it's what I think I deserve.

Maybe I'm just curious.

Maybe I tell myself I can help him.

On our first night together, he grabs a huge bowie knife out of the kitchen drawer and stalks outside with the grace of an assassin because he hears a noise. When I tell a friend this story, I laugh about it. The grim absurdity of it. The danger of it.

'Yikes,' my friend says.

'I know,' I say.

I am not the unsuspecting frog. I am German physiologist Friedrich Goltz probing the slippery skin of a frog. I am cutting it open, prodding it, scooping it hollow, boiling it in a kettle, seeing what's left. I am seeking the anatomy of a soul. What I discover is a metaphor.

VI. PLUVIANUS

The Egyptian plover is unmistakable in appearance. Its wings and long, spindly legs are blue-gray like overcast. Its chest is bright orange. It has black markings around its eyes and head, like a little bandit. It looks like a winter sunrise, a faded watercolor painting. Elegant but obtuse. Oblong but precise.

The Egyptian plover is unmistakable in appearance but most people have no idea what it looks like.

The Egyptian plover is the only member of the genus *Pluvianus*.

VII. TWO KINDS OF BROADS

Pauly says to me one day, 'There's two kinds of broads. Ones who want to be babied and ones who want to get slapped around.' Guess which kind he thinks I am.

Two nights of every week, I am not allowed to come over. At first Pauly claims he just needs a break from me, but I start finding stuffed animals in the bed. I start wondering if he's been married, if he has a kid. I say, 'It's okay if you have a kid.' He laughs it off. I get more serious. He says, 'My friend Carly's been coming over but come off it, it's no big deal.'

The admissions keep tumbling out as though they're not admissions at all. The way he tells me things, it's like he finds it trite and boring that 1) I would ask, and 2) I don't already know.

I am a lot of things, but I am not stupid. I am quick to frustration when treated as such.

He gets drunk and yells.

I back down. I simmer.

Pauly is nothing if not an authoritarian and I hate authority on principle. *Listen here buddy, I've heard punk rock before so don't you try to be quick with me.*

I tell myself I can take it.

The more he yells, manipulates, sets rules, the more I show them up as arbitrary. I snoop around his things. I make a point to open the chest behind the couch where he keeps all the shit from his time in the Marines. I read the desperate letter his mom wrote to his superiors when he went missing. I run my fingers over her loopy, schoolteacher's cursive. I make a mess of his papers and photos, make a point of letting him know I was here.

When he comes home, he's not angry. He puzzles me this way, he's always angry about the strangest, most arbitrary things. The probably very big things like this, he just squints and looks at me funny.

He says, 'I just don't understand why you find that stuff interesting.'

Carly has left her stuffed animals behind for something like the tenth time. This time, she not only made the bed with five of her stuffed toys carefully displayed in an odd tableau across the pillows, but tucked one in bed under the sheets. On my side. Or, very likely, her side.

This feels like A Move. She is making her presence known.

It begins to feel like some kind of game, like we're wrapped up in a paranormal mystery and have to talk to each other through messages in steam on the bathroom mirror.

I uncoil her long, stringy blond hairs from Pauly's hairbrush, pillows, his bar of soap. I bring over a photo of me grinning in a bassinet and hang it above the TV. I bring the photo my grandmother took on my fourth birthday where I'm wearing a red velvet dress. I still remember its satin lining whispering across my body, my grandmother's crepe paper hands braiding two full-bloomed roses into my hair before pressing the shutter release. I set this one on Pauly's bedside table, where I know Carly will have to see it every night. Morse code for codependents.

I look around the house for more clues of her. In the kitchen, I see a Sesame Street sippy cup. Odd. In the downstairs bathroom, under the sink, I find a light-up toothbrush.

I decide that Pauly must have kids I don't know about. I start wondering how old Carly is and if Pauly's maybe divorced or maybe he's still technically married and that's why he won't tell me anything. I start coming up with reasons why this is okay. He's been through a lot. He's afraid of losing me. I'm just too young and he wants to protect me in his own paternalistic and misguided way. Fine.

But then I find a shirt. Women's large. A sports bra. B-cup. A thong.

Then I find a little pink pacifier. Mixed signals.

Then I find a pack of adult diapers in the back of his closet.

It's hard to be upset at anything so absurd but I am. And once again Pauly's response is low-key. Like *what's the big deal.* Like *yeah I have an adult baby girlfriend who I shave and bathe and put a diaper on but we love each other and she's my friend, get over it.*

Yeah I shave and bathe and put a diaper on her to make her cum but we're not doing anything sexual.

I'm driving away from his house one day when I find another one of Carly's long blond hairs strung through my shirt like sutures. It's like I can't get away from her.

VIII. FEAR AS A LOVE LANGUAGE

I am not the unsuspecting frog. I am not a damsel in distress. I am not a masochist.

I ask more and more about Carly. I want to know what she's like and why Pauly won't let me go if he has her. After another spectacular fight, when I have the energy to throw some shit back his way and slam some doors, I ask what she's like when he yells.

'She just gets quiet and sits there,' he says.

I watch him fidget. He isn't looking at me.

'She's a good girl,' he mutters. 'She's just a fucking idiot. She doesn't know how to do anything. She's an idiot.'

I am sure he talks about me with her, too. He must have a lot of unsavory things to say about both of us. But I can tell that where she's *a good girl*, I'm supposed to be the smart one. The banshee. The shrew.

I'm not a girl. I'm a cunt.

I'm the one he takes to Thanksgiving with his folks because I can lie through my teeth. I'm his date for the Christmas party because I pull off May–December in an appropriate cocktail dress. I talk back and say no. I fuck your dad in style. I pack my shit and slam the door. I drive too fast just because I can. I act out at the function just because I can. I make you miss me just because fuck you. I toss back my whiskey and light my own cigarettes. I snort crushed Oxy on your counter. I'm ready to wreck your life. I'm the one you can't keep up with. I'm the one that runs outside screaming 'KIDFUCKER' while Pauly's neighbors are trying to mind their own business.

When he snaps, 'Do you want to catch a beating?' I'm the one that snaps back, 'Fucking hit me motherfucker, try it.'

I know how to fight, he fights dirty, and I don't like to lose.

That's why he keeps me around. Because he's drawn to bad behavior and hopeless nihilism. He likes a hard bitch.

Just like me, danger turns him on.

IX. LEECHES

Greek historian Herodotus wrote of the crocodile bird that it lands inside a Nile crocodile's mouth, dislodging debris and leeches from between the predator's teeth.

This is called *cleaning symbiosis.* The bird gets a free feeding and the crocodile gets a free dental. Nobody has to die.

But the crocodile bird doesn't exist.

While the bird described in Herodotus's writing has been identified as the Egyptian plover, no evidence exists to suggest that it has any such relationship with the crocodile. In fact, the phenomenon of *cleaning symbiosis* wherein a pair of interspecies animals enjoy a mutually beneficial relationship is still debated among biologists. Viewpoints on these types of interspecies relationships vary from purely mutual to purely parasitic.

Regardless, Herodotus's crocodile bird has been subsumed into a larger popular culture. Where factual basis may have failed remains metaphor. The facts don't matter. The Egyptian plover doesn't matter, its distinctive plumage doesn't matter.

No one's even heard of a plover, but *crocodile bird* means something.

I am struggling to find the benefit of knowingly perching inside a crocodile's mouth. I am struggling also to unlearn it.

X. FLOWERS

I tell myself I can take it.

When he explodes suddenly over dinner, I jump in my seat. A reflex. He turns to look at me and laughs. Sometimes he seems to snap just to remind me how bad things might get. It doesn't get bad this time, though.

I tell myself I can take it.

A searing pain is melting down my shin. He says, 'Baby did I scare you?' He says, 'Baby sit down, everything's fine.' He laughs.

A chunk of my knee is on his dining table.

I'm bleeding.

'You're bleeding,' he says. He laughs.

I tell myself I can take it.

He's ranting again. He says, 'I told you not to wear that fucking lotion. All those bullshit essential oils. What are you a fucking hippie. Stupid cunt.'

Yesterday he said, 'I love how you smell.' It smells like flowers when I leave a room. It reminds him of his mom. But today his skin is acting up. He says, 'The cream isn't working thanks to you.'

I tell myself I can take it.

He is grabbing me by the wrist and shaking a bottle of household cleaner in my face. He shoves it at me, curls my limp hand around its neck. He shakes a rag at the doorknob and says, 'Scrub. Get to it you little bitch. Get rid of all that fragrance, it's fucking up my immune system.'

I am definitely not crying.

He barks more orders. 'Scrub every surface you touched with your filthy little hands. Look what you do to me. Look what you do to me you fucking cunt.'

When my friend calls, I am definitely not crying.

When she asks why I stay, I tell her I can take it.

He is tender with me.

I am lying limp on the couch. I am crying. He sets his drink down and says, 'Baby what's the matter.' His voice is soft. He says, 'Baby why are you crying.'

I can't seem to say. I don't seem to know. I can't find my voice. The tears are traveling down my face in long, quiet streams. Everything feels far.

I am trying not to think.

He takes my hand and kisses it, barely. So softly. It's all I can take. He knows it's all I can take. I am trying not to crumple.

He keeps asking what's wrong.

I am trying not to know what I know.

His gaze is soft. He bends over me and kisses strands of my hair. Kisses my cheeks. My nose. He says, 'Close your eyes.' He kisses my eyelids and sweeps the tears away.

He says, 'I know.' His voice is shaky.

He says, 'I'm trying to change.'

He takes a sip of his drink and offers me a taste.

I do love him. This is the hardest part to say.

I love him but I just can't take it.

My friend Olivia texts, *I feel like you've been totally ditching me for some guy.*

She tells me I've been a shitty friend.

She's right.

I call a crisis hotline from a parking lot. It's cool out for summer and there's little noise. It's a Sunday. Pauly blew up at me again over nothing. I'm shaking in the driver's seat with my foot on the gas pedal and the engine turned off. The operator asks what's going on and I tell her about my boyfriend.

She takes a long pause as I sneak rabbit breaths through an outstretched hand over my mouth. She says in an icy tone, 'I can't help you if you keep going back to someone who hurts you.'

She says, 'Why should I help someone who's just going to waste it?'

I hang up in tears and watch people slowly filter out of the grocery store. I hear the lazy creak of their carts, their scattered laughter and mumbling. Teenagers on the phone, the cadence of their chatter like popping gum. Moms cooing or tugging at their kids. Haggard middle-aged men in a serious hurry.

There are so many people in the world. How did I get to be so lonely?

One day my mother says to me, 'You ruined our family.'

I promise my latest therapist Frank I'm not going to kill myself. I say, 'Please don't call the ambulance, I can't go through that again.' But why does it have to hurt so bad. What did I do to deserve this. Why is this happening to me. I am crying so hard I feel feral. Like a wounded animal, wailing and wailing. There is nothing I want. There is no plan or hope. Only despair.

I say, 'Whatever I did I'm sorry. I'm sorry so please just make it stop. Please god make it stop. I can't do this anymore.'

His brow quivers with tension as he watches me and I wonder if anything could have prepared him for this. I wonder if he goes home after our sessions and looks at his daughter differently, with this huge and soaring fear that leaps through time. Maybe this is the moment his career changes. Maybe as he watches me break down, helpless to myself, he is counting all the ways he could have done things differently. Maybe he wonders what he should have said about Pauly months ago, how the hell he could have seen this coming, how the hell writing that to-do list together would have gotten me out of this shattered, sunken place.

'My mother was right,' I say. 'Everybody was right. I ruin everything.' I say it over and over. 'I should be dead. I should be fucking dead. I don't deserve to be alive.' My nails dig into my elbows as I pretzel into an impossible knot, my body locking into a tight collapse. I say, 'I am so, so sorry.' Over and over I say, 'I am so sorry.' I know this is too much, this is just too, too much. This sadness is like hunger. This sadness is a black hole. This sadness is a bottomless wound. No one should have to see this. I'm sorry, I'm sorry, I wish I could stop.

Frank looks more human than he ever has sitting in that chair. His brow shines with sweat and the skin of his face grows taut with concern.

He leans forward and says, 'Please don't be sorry.'

He tells me he has to call an ambulance. It's a legal obligation and his hands are tied.

He says it like an apology.

When one of the paramedics asks for people to contact I recite Pauly's number without hesitation. Part of me feels like maybe he'll finally understand what he's doing to me. Another part of me feels like maybe I will finally understand what he's doing to me. I call every day from the day room of the hospital, standing side by side with other patients against the cold plaster wall. We stand there airing all our shame into the room, gazing out through floor-to-ceiling plate glass into the hall where even lonelier peers shuffle aimlessly in cheap hospital-issue socks with sticky treads. Sometimes we stand there like the firing squad is coming, cords coiled tightly around our limbs as we ready ourselves to the cold, echoing beat of the phones' ringing. Many of us weep openly against the wall, heavy black receivers pressed tenderly to our faces. Some of us never get an answer. Most of us don't get the answers we want, be it a stuffed animal or a particular book or news about a certain person. I beg Pauly to visit but he never does. He says he has a meeting, he's got a family thing, his car's acting up.

He says he can't, he can't, he can't.

He says maybe he doesn't want to.

When I'm discharged, I'm assigned a psychiatrist who puts me on mood stabilizers. The minute I get my prescription filled, I go home to Pauly. He watches me fill a weekly pill sorter. He hears the pills rattle in my purse when I walk by and says, 'Baby, you're like a pharmacy on wheels.'

I'm laughing but I don't think I like that. He grins and shakes his glass at me for a refill. Sometimes he says, 'Baby that's way too much water in there.' Sometimes he cracks a crooked smile and tells me the whiskey's just right. At the end of the night he says, 'Why don't we do a toast?' I know what the doctor said about mixing booze with my medication but I can't get myself to care. Pauly looks so happy right now.

I let Pauly pour me a Crown Royal, which I request neat. I knock it back quick and slam the glass down. It's too sweet to hold on my tongue.

'Whoa, easy slugger,' he says, like calming a spooked horse. 'Sip it. Nice and slow.'

I have two more glasses of whiskey. I have more on Saturday, Sunday, the next weekend, and the next. I sip like he tells me to.

After Pauly blows up again, over some minor flub with the groceries, I flush my pills down the toilet. If they're working, I can't tell.

A few weeks after I leave the hospital, my caseworker asks me if I'm still living with Pauly.

'He is clearly a danger to your well-being,' she says. 'I need to know that you have a safe place to go.'

I think about my parents' basement for a moment and the time I tumbled down the stairs because I was all doped up. How I fell asleep there on the floor, too beat and ashamed to call anybody. How my mother kept asking about my limp and I snapped at her the third time. How she doesn't ask me much anymore. How many times my father's thumb has hovered over the *delete* key when I've texted him begging for help. How many times I've called a hotline instead of knocking on his door. How many times I've sat at breakfast with the two of them, unable to say anything because I love them too much to open my mouth and ruin it.

I think about Ronnie's smoked-out ranch house full of screaming grandkids.

I think about Olivia's last text.

I think about Kevin and the loaded handgun he keeps in his holster and the way two tours in Iraq and Afghanistan changed him.

I tell her I'll be okay and drive to the grocery store. Pauly wants a roast chicken tonight.

hey man, i'm wondering if you can help me out. i'm writing about the whole process of leaving [redacted]. i'm trying to plot it all out: being raped, getting pregnant, the abortion, leaving his house and making impulsive decisions, staying with friends, almost dying of alcohol poisoning/low blood sugar on fourth of july 4 days after the abortion, meeting bryan 3 days after that, [redacted]'s harassment after that and so on.

i can tell the underlying "theme" is codependency and the desperate fear of being alone. i can tell it's kind of a story about coping with trauma through manic energy and restlessness. it's kind of about how miraculous it is that i survived despite being a huge bumbling mess with no direction.

it's just i've been real fucked up since revisiting this manuscript and it's probably why the book is still unfinished in the first place. it's hard accessing a lot of the memories because i've blocked so much out. i've spent so much time being in denial and refusing to talk about any of it that i'm at a loss when it comes to doing just that. i think the writing itself is fine, it's just my brain is scrambled and i can't get my story or feelings straight right now.

they say what doesn't kill you makes you stronger but that's such bullshit, y'know. i can honestly tell i'm not as smart or functional because so much of my cognitive ability's been damaged by abuse. i dunno man, do you have any ideas? is this weird? sorry if this is weird

.

FLOWERS ARE FOR PUSSIES

It's like the autofocus has malfunctioned.

One minute I am telling him I'm finished. No more bull-shit. I am telling him to *get bent motherfucker*. I'm telling him I'm done being his cum dump. I am telling him not to touch me and he is asking where I am trying to go at this hour. 'It's too late to be driving,' he says, 'you're too upset to be driving.' He says, 'Just lie down with me and we'll talk in the morning.' He says, 'Where are you trying to go.' There is nowhere to go.

I am lying down. I am rolling over on my side and pull-ing away from his smothering kiss. I don't even want to look at him. He says, 'Don't be like that.' He is grabbing me by the hips and I'm saying, 'Stop.' He is tugging at my pants. He is grabbing me by the hips and it's like the autofocus has malfunctioned. The wiring has frayed. It's like my eyes are going to be adjusting to the dark forever. Everything goes

113

soft. The light goes dim. I am drifting across a long stretch of road miles and miles from here, the car is so much bigger than my bones and I feel impenetrable inside its metal frame, shooting down a freeway in the screaming heat of July with a lit cigarette in my hand, huge and steeled on the concrete, a darting blip in the Milky Way's eye. No one can see me from space. I am making the right sounds. I'm going to know this is rape but not now. He is carving into me and I wonder how many times this has happened before.

I am making the right sounds. There is nowhere to go. I am making this okay.

I wish I was big but so what.

He is doing whatever he wants.

No one can see you from space.

FRIDAY, JUNE 6

Max grabs her towheaded five-year-old by the bicep. 'Stop that,' she says, twisting him close to her chest. 'Do you want a sternum rub?' He is screaming. She digs a bent knuckle into his chest and rubs, hard, like stubbing out a cigarette. He is screaming.

When she lets go, he gazes off at the horizon. Momentarily dazed, he shakes it off and saunters back to the sandbox by his brother. He splays his legs in the cold wet sand.

Max claps a hand on her forehead and presses it gently like she's checking her temperature. 'I just can't fucking do this anymore,' she says.

A rare summer breeze whistles through the playground. We look across the street at her parents' house. There are rows of tin-box houses on all four sides of us. Empty trucks sit in driveways and on the shoulders of quiet roads.

I ask where she wants to go for lunch and she doesn't say anything. There's little to say when there are a million things you're trying to not talk about.

Like how you can be so surrounded and alone at the same time. How the open air can feel so taut. How you can be so impossibly lodged in a place, a moment, a feeling, and yet feel so removed. How the only difference between marriage and divorce is enough. How the only difference between woman and mother can be a mistake. How the only difference between miscarriage and abortion is want.

Max says, 'He was supposed to pick up the kids two hours ago.'

I say nothing. I am three weeks pregnant.

SATURDAY, JUNE 21

My hair is falling out in clumps. My gums are going soft.

The TV mumbles inside the house. We sit in these rickety old office chairs Pauly keeps in his garage. When I roll too close to his truck, he snaps his fingers and points like he's correcting a dog. I imagine that hot day when Pauly lost it at the tollbooth. I picture him throwing his truck in reverse with gritted teeth, seething for a moment with his hand on the gear shift before jerking it into drive and pressing the pedal to the floor.

I like to think I'm a hard bitch. That nothing gets through. That I would never, ever, take this shit. And I'd like to think I never would again. I know better, though.

I hate to admit it but I am so broken down. I spend most of my time in bed. I can barely put a thought together, let alone a meal, an outfit, a grocery list.

I like to think I'm better than this. As if being hurt or not is some practical measure of worth. I know better. I know.

Each time Pauly explodes, each time he takes whatever he wants, I drift to a quiet place. In this quiet place I am shooting through space. I am big and I do whatever I want. My thoughts jam up and spark. I am not making memories, I'm hurtling through them.

The ice in Pauly's whiskey crackles like an old record, chattering against the glass as he swirls it. When he takes a drag off his cigarette and says, 'Baby we can't do this,' I say nothing.

He says, 'I don't have anything to offer a fuckin kid.'

He says, 'I drink too much.'

He says, 'My temper.'

He says, 'I get it from my father.'

He says, 'I'm never gonna change.'

He says, 'What do you want from me.'

I say nothing. I'm crying. I don't know what I was thinking. I'm laughing. I don't know what I'm thinking.

He says, 'I'm sorry.'

He says, 'What do you want from me.'

I take his whiskey and knock it back. The ice slides back in place.

He doesn't tell me to sip this time. He offers me a cigarette.

FRIDAY, JUNE 27

Pauly looks bigger in his leather jacket. His shadow looms like a storm cloud. He holds an arm out between me and the picketers. I want to turn and spit at them but he is guiding me quickly to the door. He won't hold my hand but he will hold the door open.

We sit in the waiting room. He points to one of the other couples and says, 'I wonder how many times they've been here.' I say, 'I wonder if they love each other.' He says nothing.

I ask if we can get lunch somewhere out here. I've only been to Aurora once before. He says, 'Why the hell would we want to do that?'

I begin to crumple. He grimaces and says, 'Stiff upper lip baby.'

He says, 'Come on, stop crying.'

He says, 'You're making a scene.'

The nurse hands me a form to fill out as I ask about the pain. She tells me I'll be prescribed Vicodin. 'Are you allergic to any of the following,' she reads from the form. I am doing calculations in my head. If I sit through the cramps stone-cold sober I can save the pills and go on a three- or four-day bender. She is on to the next question. I notice there is a box to check for being coerced into an abortion but there is no box to check for being coerced into pregnancy.

After undressing, I hoist my legs into the stirrups and wait for the ultrasound. The paper gown crinkles with my breath.

I think about what it will be like to spend the weekend at Pauly's. Lying back on the bare mattress in his guest room, buzzed on painkillers with the door closed as he shouts at the TV like nothing's different. Drinking again, like nothing's different. I imagine scraping up against the white walls when I stagger out for a glass of water. The rough tan washcloths when I lather blood away. I wonder if he'll be any different this time. Maybe he will heat up soup and bring it to me. Maybe he will even sit with me. Maybe he will let me pick a movie. Maybe he will bring me flowers.

I think about getting in my car and driving. There's nowhere to go but there's nowhere to be anymore, either. I think about going to that shitty dive bar on Rand in the middle of the afternoon and drinking way too fast and picking twenty songs on the jukebox. I think about calling up Pat. I think about getting a tattoo, any tattoo. Pauly hates tattoos.

I think about following picketers to their cars and slashing their tires.

It's strange how hopelessness opens you up to endless possibilities.

The doctor tells me how everything will feel before it happens. 'It's going to be cold,' she says and it is. 'There's going to be some pressure,' she says and there is. I'm crying but I make no noise. We don't make much eye contact. She doesn't make me look at the screen and she doesn't tell me if there's a heartbeat. She says it's early enough that we don't need a D&C. She says it's just a few pills. Just a few days in bed. Just a few golf-ball size blood clots.

I am crying but I make no noise. She hands me a tissue. She says, 'You can get dressed now.'

I am twenty-four years old.

No one's ever given me flowers.

On the drive back into town, I break down. I lean against the passenger side window like a ragdoll. Tears run between my cheek and the cool relief of glass. Pauly says, 'Stop crying, why are you crying.'

I say, 'Where do you think we're coming from?'

He pounds the dashboard with his fist. I choke on my breath and make a desperate grab for the door handle. He locks the doors of his truck and shouts, 'What the fuck are you doing you maniac!' His voice thunders in my ear. I am frantically tugging the handle of the passenger side door, slamming an open palm against the window again and again. 'Let me out,' I sputter. 'I have to get out of here.'

Pauly's eyes are darting to the cars around us. The engine roars as he hastily changes lanes, speeding past other drivers.

'You're making me look bad,' he shouts. 'They think I'm hurting you.'

'You are hurting me,' I say.

'They're gonna call the police,' he shouts. 'You're being a fucking lunatic.'

'Let me out,' I plead with him. 'Please let me out.' I keep trying the door. I know it's locked but I keep trying.

He says, 'You look like a fucking idiot.'

I keep mouthing, 'Let me out.'

I've worn myself out sobbing in Pauly's car. He's shouted himself calm. We walk inside and hang up our coats in silence. He glances at the clock. Normally he would be at work until five. He reminds me that he took the day off for me but I'm already heading upstairs. Halfway up, Pauly stops me to ask if I'd like to sit with him, maybe watch a movie, and I surprise myself by saying no. He says, 'Really, your pick.' For once, I don't jump at the offer. I won't jump at anything again.

'That's alright,' he says. 'You can cry all you want up there. You're safe.'

I'm already done crying.

SATURDAY, JUNE 28

Pauly is watching the news downstairs while I lie flat on my back in the guest room. The shiny polyester threads of the bare mattress catch on my blouse and skin. By now I'm used to the cramping, which doesn't make it hurt less. I run my hand over the fastidious stitching in his grandmother's quilt. I touch the warm walnut finish of the headboard, the matching dresser and nightstand. I roll the drawer of the nightstand open and closed. It's summer but this room is always cold. There's nothing on the walls. Nothing in the drawers. Pauly doesn't have a lot of guests. He doesn't have a lot of friends. The room is just white. White like a fever dream. White like a sudden shooting pain. What a waste, these beautiful antiques, this sturdy wood. What a waste, this lovingly stitched quilt. What a waste, this spacious home.

What a waste, all this love.

In the evening, the glow of my second Vicodin swells and recedes, swells and recedes with my breath as blood gushes between my legs. My insides twist and clench. I remember what Ronnie said. *There ain't no such fuckin thing as a pain-killer.* There really fucking ain't.

Pauly knocks on the door while letting himself in. Parents do the same thing, they knock as they let themselves in. The guise of permission. He glides in and sets a bowl of soup down on the nightstand.

He stands there awkwardly, like his hands are too big to handle and he doesn't know where to put them.

I take a real good look at him. I drink him in like we're meeting for the first time all over again.

He has a shitty haircut because he's too homophobic to even show the barber a picture of another man and say, 'I want that.' His clothes are plain. Beige, tan, gray, white. His hair is mousey gray. His teeth are gray. His eyes are red-rimmed with drink, his skin ruddy and pockmarked all down his cheeks and chin.

I search his face. For what, I don't know. All I know is I don't find it.

'I thought you should eat something,' he says.

I say, 'Okay.'

He lingers. He stands there like he's waiting for something. I know what he wants but he won't get it. He won't ask how I'm feeling because men like him don't know how. And it's not my job to teach them anymore. I quit. I let him stew in the heavy silence. Monday, I will pack up my things. I will have a handful of Vicodin left. I'm good at being uncomfortable. I will drive down to Oak Park and spend the night at Max's. I will drink whenever I want. I will fuck whoever I want. I will do whatever the fuck I want.

He says, 'I'll be downstairs if you need me.'

And I don't.

Here I am. Closing the door behind him and tucking myself back in bed. Letting the soup go cold. Clutching myself in pain.

This is possibility.

NO CIGAR

I.

Fourth of July. Three days since the bleeding stopped. I've been staying with Max and Kevin since the abortion. Pauly's still texting, calling, emailing. I'm doing my best to ignore it and every once in a while Max says something—'Dude, you have to just put it away. Block his number. Get a new email address.' I keep telling her I refuse to change yet another thing for him.

I sleep on their couch, watch their kids. Smoke weed with Kevin in the basement while he avoids his chores, his kids, his wife, my friend. The two of them are fighting a lot, or rather they're just not getting along. They're trying out different things. Attending sex conventions. Setting date nights. Non-monogamy.

They're throwing a party to blow off some steam. In the evening, these big dudes in tank tops and cargo shorts stroll in with hotdog buns and condiments, twelve-packs of cheap beer, bottles of whiskey with novelty shot glasses. Max and Kevin are former Marines, and most of their friends are Marines.

We're sitting in the living room, the music humming against the soles of our feet. People are hooking up in the corners of the room like nobody else is around. Once in a while, one of the kids gets loose, tearing through the room to squeal and point at the spectacle. I watch Max and Kevin glare at each other, looking up from their respective hookups and entering a minutes-long stalemate until one of them slams a cup down and corrals the kid back into bed. Everyone is shouting and laughing but all I hear are crass punch lines through the wall of noise. The jokes are otherwise lost on me.

I usually hate parties but I'm too buzzed on Vicodin to worry about what anybody's saying. I'm just laughing. About what, it doesn't matter. I haven't laughed in weeks. I look at all these fucking Marines. A lot of us went to high school or junior high together. Most of them are dropping out of school after seeing brutal combat just to pay for classes. Most of them are unemployed and addicted to something. Most of them live with their parents. They're all either single or having serious relationship problems. It's probably hard to give a fuck about anything after you've had to shoot to kill.

Every single person in this room has PTSD.

The party's winding down inside and Max is cleaning up. I'm out in the backyard smoking cigarettes with Kevin and his friends. I've had too much vodka. Too much weed. Too much Vicodin. Not enough food. I got the spins and I'm vomiting, like projectile vomiting across the backyard. Kevin goes, 'You good dude?'

And I say something like, 'Oh wow uh oh.'

I can't feel my hands. My vision's blacking out. 'Let's get you inside,' Kevin says. He guides me by my wrist and the small of my back. 'I'm sorry,' I say, 'I'm sorry I can't walk.' I'm laughing. Nobody else is laughing.

Max rushes over and asks what's wrong. I'm stumbling and laughing. Kevin says, 'I don't know, she just puked real hard and she's like shaking.' The house is dim. The TV shines blue light in the room. Nobody else is laughing.

I'm being carried to the couch. I say, 'I'm sorry I'm such a mess.'

Someone says, 'Jesus Christ this is fucked.'

'I ruined the party,' I say.

Someone says, 'I can't deal with this.' Someone says, 'The fuck is wrong with you, she's gonna die.'

'My sugar,' I say. 'I haven't eaten today.'

'She said she's diabetic or something.'

'How much did you let her drink.'

'She's a grown-ass adult I don't know.'

'Kevin her sugar's crashing. Kevin watch her.'

'Keep your eyes open, dude. Open your eyes.'

'Jesus what did she take.'

'Her lips are turning blue oh fuck.'

My breath is ragged and I'm so cold. My teeth are chattering. Everything is going black. I think if I just close my eyes this will all be over. No more crying. No more regret. No more responsibility. No more hospitals. No more Pauly. No more guilt trips. No more itchy loneliness.

Someone is holding my head. Someone is saying my name. 'Sung. Have some water. Open your mouth.'

Everyone towers over me, their features blurred in the darkness. I'm surrounded by their suffocating presence, stretched tall by the blue light of the TV.

No more laughter. No more music.

Max frantically rubs my hands and arms. She is trying to make fire. She says, 'Wake up. Don't go to sleep. Wake up.' Her long curly hair brushes against my eyelids as she lightly slaps my cheek, like a nurse bringing a vein to life. She's reaching into a paper bag. She sticks her finger into my mouth and it tastes sweet. She says, 'We need to get your sugar up.'

This huge breath tears through me like a semi truck. I can't move but I can see. Kevin is crouched on the floor, clutching a bag of powdered sugar in his arms as his wife forces it down my throat. His eyes are wide. I can tell he doesn't want to look but he can't look away. His tense hands crumple the paper bag. I've never seen him like this before.

I say, 'I'm sorry. I am so, so sorry.'

'Just stay with us,' he says, shaking his head. 'Don't fucking leave me dude.'

II.

July 6. It's a perfect summer day. Olivia and I haven't hung out in a while, though not for lack of trying. At least on her end. She's been texting me every day while I've been busy having an abortion and sleeping on people's couches and almost dying.

We're sitting on the floor of her childhood bedroom, our eyes wandering up the walls and gliding over her trinkets as we make chitchat and politely hide our boredom.

I'm trying to remember what it is you *do* with people.

I remember being with her last summer. I remember wearing a white thrift store dress with navy flowers, and Olivia wearing this soft blue polka dotted strapless number. We're dressed up for a Fourth of July luncheon, just the two of us in her mom's garden. 'Eight bucks on clearance,' she boasts. We've made ice cream cake and olive tapenade to eat on fancy crackers. We're sitting in the hot sun. We don't have a lot of other friends. The cat grazes our bare legs. There's something desperate about the way we keep saying, 'This is *so* good,' our forks scraping the plates and jarring us out of our sleepy complacency. Olivia flips through channels with white knuckles coiled around the remote. Searching for what, she doesn't know. All she knows is it *has* to be *just right*. We talk over the show as a fat bumblebee bounces off the screen door and ice cubes slouch with the heat in our untouched glasses. We talk and talk without saying much of anything. 'Oh I saw this really good show just came out on Netflix,' 'Oh have you tried that vegan diner in Logan Square,' 'Oh I've been trying those adult coloring books to keep busy,' and the beats of silence sting even woven together with the ricochet of the TV's infomercial pep.

It's always been like this with her. Tense.

Today we sit in Olivia's childhood bedroom pressing our palms into the plush carpet, spitballing things we could do with this *lovely, lovely day* as if we're really going anywhere to do anything. I'm trying to remember what it is you *do* with people. Olivia combs through her thick brown hair with trembling fingers. Her eyes are shifty when I look at her. She clears her throat when our eyes meet as if to say, 'Excuse me. *Excuse* me.'

She says, 'So are you going back to school in the fall?'

'Yeah, I guess I gotta,' I say.

I spot a plastic bottle on the desk behind her. It's white and stout, about the size and shape of a soda can. Stickered by a pharmacist.

I say, 'Hey can I get a glass of water.'

'No,' she jokes. She gets up and laughs dryly, as though relieved or even grateful for a reason to leave the room. She shuts the door behind her with the kind of delicacy you'd use stacking the roof on a house of cards. She always moves slowly, walks on the balls of her feet like she's scared of breaking something, everything.

I reach over and pick the bottle up off the desk. I turn it over in my clammy hands. It's the biggest bottle of Klonopin I've ever seen.

I dump half of it out into my purse.

III.

Over OkCupid messages, I agree to meet this guy at a sushi bar and he gives me his phone number. His name is Bryan, he's thirty-nine years old, and by his grainy photo I can tell he's probably not hideous. The first thing I text him is, *do you do drugs?*

He types for a long time. He stops typing. He starts typing again. Finally he sends a simple *yes.*

That night, he takes me to his mom and stepdad's house. Two dogs run up from the basement to greet me. He leads me down there, where he sleeps, and they pitter-patter behind us. There are a bunch of amps, bass guitars, a microphone, some bongo drums. Two big easels. Book shelves lined with art history tomes and Buddhist texts. It's dim, and a little swampy. The dogs lie on the floor, rolling slightly on their sides to look at us with their tongues lolling out.

Against one wall, there's this little shrine made of driftwood. I'm touching his singing bowl. I'm picking up and putting down a meditation wheel. I'm rubbing ash off a cone of incense. He says, 'Just so you know, I'm a Buddhist. So don't worry. I won't hurt you. It goes against my beliefs.'

I laugh. 'Man I don't give a fuck,' I say.

'I'm just letting you know you're safe.'

I laugh harder. 'Look, I'm taking a calculated risk,' I say. 'People will say anything. But your mom knows we're here. You got nice dogs.'

He taps a little cocaine out onto an album cover and cuts it into a line with his debit card. I watch him lick the card hungrily.

I tell him I've never tried coke before and he says, 'I'll make sure you don't do too much.'

He lays out a line for each of us and says, 'Ladies first.' I snort both of them and say, 'I don't know what happened.' This happens several times.

He says, 'I could've sworn I cut two.'

'I don't know,' I say, 'I don't remember.' And I kind of don't. Years later I'm still not convinced that I was this greedy. I'm also on so much Klonopin that I can't stop grinning and my breath is shallow and wispy.

'I'm not making a move tonight,' he says. 'I know I brought you here but I don't expect anything.'

I kiss him.

He says, 'You don't have to do that.'

'Do you want me to stop,' I say.

He laughs quietly.

I'm sitting next to Bryan on the back porch, starting to sober up. I hate this feeling. I'm running out of Klonopin already. I hate feeling. He lights two cigarettes and hands one to me. I say, 'You know I had an abortion last week.' I've known him for three hours but what do I care if I scare him off. I'm not trying to fall in love or anything. I'm just trying not to go home.

I'm going to quit smoking. I'm going to get clean. I'm going to organize my bookshelf and get back in school. I'm going to start writing again. I'm going to start running again and eating right. I'm going to get my shit together.

I say, 'This guy's still hassling me. My ex.'

I say, 'He was so abusive but I think I've never known anything else.'

I say, 'He raped me I don't even know how many times.'

I say, 'Jesus Christ what did I do to deserve this you know, people have been shitting on me since day one you know, and I keep going back for more, I keep hoping.'

He takes a deep, quiet drag.

I say, 'But he's not a bad guy.' I say, 'I still really, really want to love everybody. I still really, really love him.'

I say, 'Everybody needs love even if they don't deserve it,' and I'm not exactly sure who I mean. I say, 'Don't you think we should all have something like love for everyone? I don't even mean in some hippie-dippie fucking free love way I just mean it's a pragmatic need in the world. But nobody else seems to feel like that and I just keep getting myself all beat up.'

I say, 'I want to live so bad. But this world is killing me.'

I don't know that I'm crying until I feel his hand on my back.

I say, 'I almost died three days ago.'

He says, 'I'm glad you didn't.'

He says, 'I have work in the morning but you don't have to leave.'

He says, 'I've never met anyone so honest.'

He says, 'I got dumped nine years ago.'

He says, 'I moved back in here and started drinking again.'

He says, 'I've just been sort of waiting to die.'

WHERE'S
THIS BITCH GOING

AFTER WEEKS OF INTERMITTENT HARASSMENT, I finally tell Pauly never to contact me again. Before I get a chance to block his number, he texts, *I'm tearing up those pics u left behind. Who knew such a cute little girl could grow up into such a fucking cunt?* He's apparently destroying the only copies of those photographs in existence. The negatives were lost someplace between here and South Korea. It feels as though I am losing another tangential link to the place I was born.

But I do block his number.

We're lying back on Bryan's bed, taking greedy gulps of water from a dusty glass. Slick with sweat and panting after another coke-fueled fuck, I look around the basement. There's a framed painting of a strange, outer space scene hanging over us, full of rocks and lonely skies and dusty reds. Across from us, a giant canvas takes up the entire wall—a powerful nude in blues and yellows and greens, its frenzied brush strokes dragging and swirling in a complex dance. On one of Bryan's easels, a portrait of a coquettish woman looking behind her, a little reminiscent of a Klimt, her features rosy and playful, hair a flowing geometry of suggestions. I have spent almost every night here since we met. When he's at work I sometimes amble around the basement floor, cold to the touch after a night of fitful sex or crying or stress dreams. I like to wander around naked and touch the canvases. I know I shouldn't. I feel like I've snuck into a museum after hours. Like I'm reading Bryan's diary. I like to stare into the eyes of his portraits and wonder what his relationship is with the people in them. How he met them, if he did. Why he chose them.

I take another gulp of water and ask, 'Who is that woman? The one looking back in that painting.'

He looks up briefly.

'Oh I don't even know that chick's name,' he says. 'She sent me a selfie for reference in a chat room. Just needed something to paint.'

I ask when he painted last and he heaves a deep sigh. 'Too long,' he says. 'Years too long.'

I turn my eyes to the dingy ceiling full of cobwebs as Bryan turns on his side, ready to fall asleep. People say the difference between cobwebs and spiderwebs is that cobwebs are old, haggard, long-vacated things. This is not true. The difference between cobwebs and spiderwebs has to do with the level of sophistication—spiderwebs are of more elegant, precise construction, whereas cobwebs are tangled and woven haphazardly, with a sticky silk that seems to melt and collapse into itself. Bryan's cobwebs are built by comb-footed spiders or sheet-weaving spiders.

The myth that cobwebs indicate a dead or missing occupant isn't altogether untrue—the types of spiders who weave these tangled, irregular cobwebs tend to have itchy feet. They often abandon a web in favor of spinning a new one.

As I look around this basement, I think about that. How many times I've gotten itchy feet. But what does this place say of Bryan? A half-made home. He's lived here for nine years, drinking alone. His canvases gathering dust. It's like he's decided to abandon this place without having someplace else to go.

Suddenly he takes my arm and wraps it around himself. I laugh.

'Is someone feeling lonely?' I say.

He grunts.

'I'm right here,' I say.

He grunts.

I turn to him and he pulls me closer by the wrist, gently but with a certain greed. He asks me to wrap my hand around his throat, not too tight, but like a nice scarf. My laughter shakes us as he hugs my arm close to his chest.

'I used to sleep like this when I was little,' he says. 'I'd hold my throat. It made me feel nice and tucked in. I always did it like this. I couldn't sleep any other way.'

'I never heard anything like that,' I say, laughing. 'You're fucking weird.'

He can only reply in soft little whimpers. He's drifting. His breath rocks me to sleep.

Bryan's eyes are green and wide. Thickly lashed and heavy-lidded like a cow's. The rest of his body is exactly forty, maybe older with all the reckless pickling and abuse it's been through, but those peepers stay boyish and sparkling with intrigue. His lips jut out, full with a sweeping bow, flushed pink especially when he drinks. He has a long, aquiline nose that lends his face what I like to call an old world dignity. His gingery beard hides a weak chin. He shrugs off compliments and can't come up with a single thing to like about his face. Especially when he drinks.

On Monday, Bryan calls up to say he's thinking of visiting his hometown of Decatur to buy a couple pork loins for the restaurant. There's a meat market down there that has a special going on, plus taxes are lower over in Macon County. He asks if I'd like to join him, make a weekend of it. Visit some of his old haunts, meet some of his old friends. It takes me a while to decide on an outfit. I don't know this guy all that well yet. But more importantly, he doesn't know me that well yet. It's a chance to be likable, really dig my hooks into someone just because I can. Play dress-up with a grab bag of personality traits. Ride the manic wave. I try on quirky and strange and a little infuriating. I try on the flighty airhead. I try on the quiet sage. I choose a thin rayon dress when I find out we're going hiking through a forest preserve. I toss a change of clothes in a tattered tote bag and pile into his car for a three-hour drive down south. I change the radio station at the pace of a hummingbird. I roll the window down all the way and stick my head out the window to breathe in the openness and stare clear across the cornfields like this is the most exciting thing on Earth. He thinks it's a riot, he even says the line I'm coaxing out of him, 'Damn,' he says, 'I never seen someone so excited by corn.' I sit smug in the easy wind-up of a long con. I'm somebody that somebody can love.

But the truth is only a shade off. Maybe it's not the corn or the soybeans. Maybe not even Bryan's droning narration about the history of Decatur—'At one time this place was a booming coal town,' he says, 'and it was going to be capital of Illinois'—maybe not the choking blue sky or the wind pressure beating against the car, the smell of hay, the stiff and faded old map stretched out on the dashboard, maybe not the rickety family businesses standing on the same corner for fifty years—'That there's the cracker pizza joint I spent mosta high school at,' Bryan says—but there's something astonishing going on. There is a moment following tragedy that some people never get to experience. You have to be ready for it or it will crush you to dust. It's like a window flung open and naked to the day. It's like being lifted away. It's like being stranded with everything you need. It's the moment you call a cornfield beautiful because you mean it, because you've never seen the world like this before, because newness no longer strikes terror but rather brings hope. You jerk awake into it like meeting yourself on a blind date. You surrender to that sudden first rush of joy without consequence, no more doom or fear or guilt, surrender to the sheer devastating presence of life, huge and indifferent, pushing into you like God's breath.

The Scovill Zoo of Decatur, Illinois, has one cheetah with missing teeth. There's a wolf trail that surrounds the perimeter of the park, fenced off with chicken wire. Bryan tells me about growing up in a house only a few miles from the zoo, how all these wild things would jump over or tunnel under the fences and pop up in his backyard. Every couple of months his mother would scan the view outside the kitchen window with the telephone cord wrapped anxiously around her wrist, and she'd call the zoo to say there's a peacock or a wolf where there shouldn't be. I imagine Bryan as a little boy, his eyes sparkling against the glare of the sun as his cereal goes soggy, dismayed when his mother tells him to stay put inside until the zookeeper's come and gone with the wild intruder, knowing there's some whole world *out there*. I imagine him sitting in that kitchen before ever sipping his first drink or snorting his first line or leaving his first pawn shop, a little boy living just on the other side of magic.

I watch mesmerized as Bryan approaches the bonobo apes and hoots in a low, husky voice. He gestures warmly with his hands, holding them open and low for the apes to see. The bonobos hoot back. At the petting zoo, Bryan gets into a friendly sparring match with a baby goat, butting his knuckle against its head and tickling its chin as reward. He seems to have an intuitive connection with these animals. Like he's on the same peaceful wavelength.

He explains that the zoo started as an educational farm in the sixties and grew quickly into a thriving attraction with the addition of more exotic exhibitions and educated staff. When funding started to fall off, the place started to go downhill. A lot of the animals were moved to better-equipped facilities, some of them died.

A lot of the specific history doesn't filter through to me. I'm too distracted by all the clucking, flapping, pitter-patter, the smells and refracting light. But I do catch Bryan heaving a long, wistful sigh. He says, 'This place isn't what it used to be.'

We look over at an emu as it bows and primps itself. It kicks its feet at me. 'Ugh, I hate that thing,' I say. 'It's kinda scary. And ugly.'

Bryan's eyes get soft and misty. 'It looks sick,' he says.

I've never been to the zoo with my boyfriend before. I've never sprawled out champagne drunk on a stiff Holiday Inn bed before. It feels like I've never been horny before. I've never wandered around the breakfast bar of a three-star hotel before, swatting flies away from the slimy lukewarm grapes and wearing sunglasses in the daytime. I don't know if it's supposed to be romantic but I do know I'm having the time of my life. Even if Bryan seems at times embarrassed by his own brokedick attempt at a weekend getaway.

This is the sleepy sad slice of America I crave as an immigrant. Like sleeping in someone else's lived-in house, like cheap real estate nobody wants, like driving past the *one* Chinese restaurant in town that isn't even good, past the cracker pizza joint, the burnt-out neon signs, mosquitoes the size of quarters rising like disease from swampy creeks.

Our last night in Decatur, we eat crumbly hamburgers in our room. He asks how I'm feeling and I tell the truth.

For my twenty-fourth birthday, Pauly hands me a gift card to Kohl's. I've never been to Kohl's.

Sifting through their racks of sensible black and gray dresses, cream chiffon blouses, easy jersey knits, I get an image of the kind of woman he wants to be fucking. She's from a conservative Roman Catholic family just like his. She breaks out her grandmother's scratch-made meatball recipe for every special occasion, but won't dare to eat more than one in a sitting. She picks up his prescriptions without being asked or asking what they're for. She consumes twelve hundred balanced calories a day and does rigorous cardio three times a week. She never talks back or slams doors or packs bags. She has neat brown hair down to her waist and she hasn't cried in six years. She doesn't even want to cum.

I don't find anything I want. I end up buying him a watch.

I don't remember how Pauly and I ended up in bed after our first date. I remember falling into his arms out of a clawing loneliness that never left. I remember that's how I felt every second of the day, lonely and estranged from myself. It feels more like a place than a memory, *the foggy place* where part of me still wanders. White and beige and gray, colorless like Pauly's townhouse. The shrouded air of this place smothering every living sound into a muffled struggle, every touch into a clammy intrusion. I don't remember the escalation of his anger. I don't remember the timeline. I remember him jerking me away when I touched his chest. He would snap his teeth and say, 'Not the heart, don't you touch me there.'

The week before I turn twenty-five, Bryan and I are lying in bed when he asks what I want for my birthday. I burst into tears and say, 'I don't even know.' I don't think I've ever answered this question. He presses his face against mine, wrapping an arm around me from behind. His soft sandy hair falls across my eyes. My fingers hook into the sheets. I say, 'Why does it matter.' I say, 'My birthday makes me feel bad. I try to be excited for Christmas too because it's what you're supposed to do but it always feels bad.' I can't seem to articulate this any better but Bryan doesn't demand coherence. He holds me in the hushed darkness. Moonlight slices through the blinds and I say, 'The shadows look like a Mondrian, don't they.' He is falling asleep. I say again, 'The shadows look like a Mondrian, don't they.' He says, 'I'm trying to stay up with you.' I am trying to stave off hope. I am running my fingers through his hair and chanting to myself what is real and what is not real. What is real: this hair, this throat, this scrape of stubble, this mattress on the floor, this nicotine stain, this hunger, this sinking, this body, his body, this bite of loneliness and dread as he drifts to sleep. What isn't real: tomorrow, and everything in it.

Dr. Claire reaches across the room and rests a hand on my shoulder. She says, 'You are going through a hard time. But it will pass.' We just met about an hour ago and during introductory questions she tapped into something a little too raw. I tell her I think my time is up and she tells me that's for her to worry about. I'm crying so hard I can't catch my breath. 'Why can't I stop?' I ask and she says, 'Try to take some deep slow breaths,' but I can't. 'Why can't I stop,' I say. 'Oh god it's just so much, why does it have to be like this, why, why, why.'

'Name something you see in the room,' Dr. Claire says. 'Can you do that?'

'The carpet. It's gray.'

'Good,' she says. 'Now name three more.'

'The light. It's warm. Orange. The calendar. It's getting dark outside.'

'What about three things you feel on your skin or in your body? Like are you hungry, does your back ache? No judgments on whether it's bad or good. Just name them.'

'My hands are cold and puffy. My clothes feel tight.' My heart is beating fast but it's beginning to slow down.

'That's very good,' she says. 'Now two things you hear.'

'I hear the clock ticking. My foot. Tapping on the floor,' I say.

I feel the thrust of our hips and the sweep of hair on the back of my neck and the safe restraint of Bryan's arm hooked around me. It smells like hot puffs of morning breath and latex. Rained-on concrete. The windows are open. I hear my mouth make noises I think I learned from porn. I still don't know how to be honest and naked at the same time.

I see Bryan's hand gripping the bed, its hairs slick with sadness. I don't know how long I've been crying and neither does he.

The restaurant eats up most of Bryan's time but he usually gets home early on Sundays because they're so dead. Sundays are for those die-hard alcoholics who drink noon to midnight. People without families to see. We're having dinner for my birthday tomorrow at a French restaurant in the ritzy part of town but he wants to do something nice tonight, too. I'm flipping through channels while he bangs around the kitchen. I ask what he's doing in there, but he doesn't hear me over the angry sizzle of a hot iron pan, the scrape of a whisk. I am teetering off the edge of the couch, balancing on the balls of my feet. My fingernails dig into the remote, the cushions, my thighs. I don't know how to be at ease. No one's ever done this for me before. He sets an oblong porcelain dish in front of me.

'So this here's a strip steak with some onion-jalapeño marmalade,' he says, 'and off to the side here you've got wilted greens and red potatoes cooked with pancetta.'

He hands me a fork and knife as I stare down at the plate in silence. He says, 'I been planning this all week. Hopefully the pancetta's not overcooked, mighta scorched some while I was checking on the steak. Sorry if the potatoes are underdone, they're not my strong suit.'

I double over.

He takes the steak knife from my limp hand and settles down beside me. I'm crying.

'What do you mean *sorry*,' I say.

I am standing in line at the bank or walking the dogs or sitting at home with the TV on when some slight noise or movement gets to me. Sometimes it's silence that sends me hurtling, sometimes it's the mention of something that reminds me of Pauly. I am plunged into the fog. The trapdoor gives out beneath me and I hang suspended in the cold damp stillness. I am lost to myself until the body breaks through to *something*. The beating of a fist against the skull. The hoarse, wretched scrape of a raw throat screaming. The smother of a pillow, the cringing tension of my joints. Violence carves my way back to body.

But Bryan's coming home now. He's going to hold me back from myself. He's going to pour me a glass of water and wash his hands at the kitchen sink to start dinner. When he senses I'm watching, he will twist his face into clownish expressions. He will ask, 'Will you be alright while I cook?'

There's a certain sunny warmth to Bryan's voice, rounded and stretched and grated by years of smoking, years of Texan life and a Decatur upbringing, molded around a lifelong speech impediment that his parents sought to amend with speech therapy he only recollects in shades of feeling—shame, inadequacy, the quiet flush of blood to his face. To this day he says *wash* like *warsh* and doesn't like it being brought to his attention.

I come home from classes and friends' homes to the chatter of an *Antiques Roadshow* marathon. Bryan gets excited about dead people's things and nostalgic about memories that aren't his. He will shake his head and say, 'They've just had a Jasper Johns sitting in their garage this whole time?' and remind me of his childhood friend whose father worked out of Andy Warhol's factory. He'll say the guy apparently has a bunch of Andy's prints sitting in the cellar. He never fails to find an opportunity to bring up this story, unfolding its familiar outlines carefully like an ancient map, lingering in it with the grave sincerity of a dying prophet with one parable to pass on. He doesn't even need to bring up the story for me to know that's the reason he's clinging to some musty old thing when I ask why he hasn't thrown it away.

Dr. Claire asks me to picture feelings and energy as the pendulum of a clock or metronome. Constant, lifelong trauma teaches our bodies to stay alert. The pendulum swings wildly from one end to the other. From devastation to screaming glee. From sleeping seventeen hours to Craigslist hookups and shoplifting. From flight to fight.

Our main goal is to teach me to honor feelings without vacillating between such extremes. To set my metronome to a reasonable tempo, respond to challenging situations with a rational, appropriate amount of energy. Put simply, I need to *chill* the *fuck out*.

Dr. Claire says I can practice this any time of day. Name four things I sense, whether it's sight or touch or smell. Then three, then two, then one. This is called a grounding exercise. She says this is something I can and very well should try even when I'm feeling perfectly okay. It's also a useful tool for de-escalation. It will get me back in the driver's seat when I'm spinning out in a fury. When things are about to get thrown or broken. When I'm ready to go screeching out of the parking lot to who knows where.

After a handful of therapy sessions, something goes wrong with our paperwork. Turns out my insurance didn't go through. Bryan and I don't qualify for Medicaid but we can't afford insurance. We can't pay for therapy and rent at the same time.

When I come to the station to pick his ass up, Bryan is huffing and puffing in full lotus position on a cot in his holding cell. I have never seen someone meditate spitefully before.

I fully hate him in this moment. All his hypocrisies and contradictions laid out like this, like someone's clothes dumped on the street in the wake of a furious breakup. I don't need to be seeing him like this. It's painfully embarrassing. Full lotus with his fucking Superman shirt on. White-knuckling the steering wheel on our way home, I think of that dusty-ass shrine in the house with its Tibetan prayer flags and singing bowl, his cracker-ass tendency to say 'namaste' in casual conversation, his convenient cherry-picking of tenets, his compulsive hoarding of possessions in complete disregard of the Buddhist principle of non-attachment. This white motherfucker playing victim when I pick him up from the drunk tank at four in the morning with all his limbs intact, no charges pressed, lying through his crooked yellow teeth with all this 'I only had one glass of wine' bullshit. Griping about 'the Police State' with booze on his breath and a slur in his speech like his tongue's hoisting bricks. He can't even walk straight, he can't even look me in the eye, he can't even say 'Thank you' let alone 'Sorry' and still he's insisting they're a bunch of fascists out to get him.

Look man ACAB or whatever but shut the fuck up.

How does a codependent tell time?

Every hour is *where are you* o'clock. And the people you're drawn to tend to be exactly the kinds of people who inspire that kind of question. The vicious cycle of attraction and reinforcement. So when I text Bryan *where are you* earlier that night, a few months into our living together, it comes as no surprise that he texts back, *I'm in a cop car hold on.* Motherfucker's in handcuffs in the back of a squad car and still texting on the sly to let me know where he's at.

Jesus fucking Christ, man.

Bryan's southern drawl comes crashing through walls when he drinks. In court, the cop who pulled Bryan over leans forward in the witness stand, his movements willowed with boredom, and he says into the mic that the defendant seemed intoxicated judging by a *thick-tongued* manner of speaking. I will remember this phrase a year later when Bryan lies to me. 'I'm not drunk, I just had a long day,' he will say. 'It was only one glass of wine,' he will say. How many times has he come home talking with that thick tongue? How many times have I let it go, how many times have I resigned myself to one of his stubborn-ass lies? So I'm stomping around the house demanding the truth. Screaming, 'You made a fool of me.' Screaming, 'How could you lie straight to my face.'

Screaming, 'I can't believe a goddamn thing you say.' I will hear his canvases shredding as my shears go through them. I will hear the blood pounding in my ears as I stomp and tear and toss. The wooden frames will combust against the walls and splinter through my skin.

'Do you hate me that much?' he will ask, his tongue like honey, like molasses, like tar.

'You call yourself an artist?' I will say. 'Act like one and make some more.' Every bit of ugliness I've swallowed I will unleash into the room in an acid flood. Every scathing truth.

How does a codependent tell time? I'm at my friend Vonn's house and we're playing cards with her roommate Tera and boyfriend Daniel. Vonn sits at the head of the table eyeing her hand with this immaculate sort of blank selfie stare like somebody might snap a picture any moment. Lipstick crisp. Blue hair styled. Eyeliner dagger sharp. Daniel plays impulsively, slapping cards down like they're on fire. He's not here to play cards, he's here to crack jokes and make Vonn's eyes roll. Tera and I look at each other with discomfort when they bicker or kiss each other. We laugh whenever Vonn puts him in his place for saying something tasteless.

Bryan hasn't texted me back in three hours but I'm thinking I should ease up and let the guy have his fun. He's playing bass at an open mic and seeing some old friends. I find myself saying this out loud. 'He's playing music, he's being social, he's drawing again. I'm proud of him.' I am saying this out loud when nobody asked. We're sitting around a table playing cards and I keep checking my phone. I'm trying to keep calm. *What do I feel, what do I see, what do I hear.* I'm doing the right thing. I'm letting my boyfriend breathe. I'm doing the grounding exercise. The room is warm with twinkly Christmas lights. My hands are clammy. My stomach feels knotted. Vonn's cat brushes up against my legs. My clothes cling to my chest and arms. There's a twitch in Vonn's smile as she says, 'It's going to be fine dude. Just try to have a good time and don't worry about his ass.'

I smell weed and beer. I hear the shuffle of cards. I see everyone's teeth, clapping together with hoarse laughter like the shutters of a stormed-out window.

Four hours since he texted back. 'I should just let the guy fucking have a life,' I say. Nobody asked. My hands are shaking. I say, 'You know what, I'm gonna call him real quick,' and all my friends are laughing about it. Our anxieties are running gags, the fodder for most of our jokes. That's how we keep going. I'm pacing down the hall as the phone rings and rings and no one is picking up so I call back and call back and I keep hitching that automated voicemail so I figure maybe it's loud at the open mic but when I look at the clock it's well past the time open mic ends. I'm calling and calling and Vonn hands me a Klonopin and I'm tapping my foot with my nails digging into my palms when the phone finally rings.

I can't even tell what the fuck he's saying. That thick tongue. Something about a parking lot. The 7-Eleven on Plum Grove. I hear his puke splatter on the asphalt.

Blood rushes to my face. 'Stay right the fuck there,' I say. 'Don't move, don't drive, just stay.' I'm gnashing the Klonopin between my teeth and running my shit out the door as my friends groan with sympathy. I'm speeding down the interstate and bashing my fist against the dash as some pop song twinkles inappropriately on the radio. My screams skid out my throat like rockets, tearing everything up. *I will not cry. I will not cry. I will not cry for you, motherfucker.*

Mary is the tallest, blondest, fittest person I know. She was a certified welder. She's a mother. She's a student. She's a poet. She laughs with her whole body and her hands seem to be made of nothing but length and tight knots. She is deeply touched by pinecones, the weather, by books and films, by colors and tastes and the smell of lavender. She's tattooed all over her freckled pink skin and she's the only one who knows what any of them mean. She cries, I imagine, in quiet, lonely bursts. She has at least a dozen different email addresses, each username equally obscure, always something like *quietclocks* or *blisswindow*. She's elusive, wily, everywhere with you and yet somehow never around in that way only people who've been *through* some *shit* can be.

Mary is the kinda bitch who won't tell you dick about her childhood or her husband or her day but she'll poke at you with little reminders all week that she's there, a meme in your DMs, a Rilke quote, a painting that reminds her of you. She's the kinda bitch who will never take up your offer of a couch to crash on while shit dies down at home but will drop everything and fishtail across the slick Midwestern ice to make sure you don't kill yourself before Christmas.

And so here she comes. Rapping at the door with her tough walnut knuckles, straw-colored hair thrown wild. I am upstairs in the living room of Bryan's mother's house, shoulders caved in and clenching my jaws so the bad things don't come tumbling out. Mary comes in like the wind. The dogs are running circles around her, woofing with their eyes bugged out. She stalks across the floor to me and says, 'Hey kiddo.'

I'm sinking into Bryan's mom's chair, where she'll spend the evening watching her shows. My knees knock together as I limply test my limbs. Mary is chattering and I don't know about what but it's not about the big bad thing that's happening. She's just standing there on her long sturdy legs like everything is fine. 'How is school going,' she asks. 'When's Bryan coming home, I'd like to meet the guy.' She stoops down to calm the dogs' incessant barking. I tell her about Bryan, how long I've been staying with him. How his mom and stepdad go down to Florida every winter and he house-sits and watches the dogs. About his annual winter depression and how he practically begged me to move in so he wouldn't have to be alone when they left. She says, 'Hey, free rent,' and we laugh about it but there's more to it that doesn't need to be said.

Mary is talking about the house and how big it is, it's so open in here, the windows are huge, the yard has a great view out to a lake. She says, 'It's no big deal, the kid's asleep and I can stay until backup's arrived.' I'm erasing my text messages. I don't want to remember all the explosive, self-destructive things I've said or to how many people. I don't want to remember Bryan's pleading, desperate replies in between tickets during the dinner rush. I don't want to have to see myself.

And it's starting to feel normal. Like Mary and I are just two pals hanging the fuck out. Like I've never cried in my life. Like I'm perfectly hydrated and I've never been raped.

But when Bryan finally gets off work and pulls into the driveway, it's hard to keep pretending. He lets the door slam shut and slides into the house like the wild card on a sit-com, a faint whiff of beer on his breath, eyes red-rimmed and chest heaving. He sees Mary, sees me, and says, 'Are you okay? Is everything okay?' We all know it's not but I can't answer that, I can't say anything or the bad things will come spilling out. I am nodding silently but now the crying is coming again and I hold it back.

'I better get home,' Mary says. She turns to face me and we lock eyes for a moment. Quieter, she asks, 'Are you sure you're all right? With him?'

I nod and thank her.

'Let me talk to you real quick,' Bryan says. He follows after Mary as she heads for the door. I hug my knees as they walk out together. I can see them through the big glass front door, the yellow light of the streetlamp shining across their faces. They are standing in the driveway and saying things about me. They are hugging. Bryan walks back in-side and sinks to his knees by my chair, resting his chin on my lap. He looks up at me, his face shining with tears.

'I'm just glad she was here,' he says. 'I'm glad someone cares about you.' His eyes are so wide, I see a vast world of fear and regret and apology in them. He says, 'I'm sorry I couldn't be here sooner.' He says it like work is a choice. He says it like there is some fix for all this. He says it like by sooner he means years ago, before Pauly, before the drugs, before, before, before.

All the air seeps from me like the long, sad, last note of an aria. Here it comes. I'm sorry, I'm so sorry, I wish I could have, I should have tried to, it's not your fault, I don't know why I'm like this. All the bad, scary, useless things pour out into the quiet room as the dogs sit and watch.

'What can I do?' he asks.

I say, 'Maybe I'll feel better if it looks more like Christmas in here.' So he turns the radio on and tunes it to the holiday station I've been blasting all month to fight off the crying jags. He grabs a couple boxes out of the basement and dusts them off with his hands. He unravels a big shimmering garland of tinsel and says, 'Y'know my mom will be thrilled we're actually using the Christmas stuff. She takes it down from the shelf every year before leaving town, just hoping I'll put it up around the house. I'm just not a Christmas person I guess.'

I turn over one of the ornaments in my hand, watching the light bounce off its shiny red paint. 'I love Christmas,' I say. 'It's the one big normal thing I want.'

I'm always mistaking need for want and love.

I wake up to the smell of chives and butter. Breakfast is cooking. My eyes are puffy from crying when I walk into the kitchen looking for Bryan. His lips are puckered in that way I love, with great focus. He does this whenever he runs around the kitchen at work, pulling tickets and ringing bells and sliding cast iron into the oven. The ease of his movement is like gravity, like a law of nature, pure muscle memory. He looks like that when we fuck.

LOVE BUG

After signing the lease to our new apartment, Bryan and I stroll into a nearby breakfast café called Jelly. It's clean and air-conditioned. There are bright walls and tablecloths and fresh-cut daisies in mottled glass vases. Sheer gauzy drapes, lots of friendly pastels. The servers wear yellow polos and talk with lots of pep. Our server pours Bryan a coffee and sets a sweaty crystal pitcher of citrus water on the table before moving on from our corner booth. My thighs squeak against the vinyl. Bryan laughs as I bounce in my seat.

'Goddamn, what a relief,' Bryan says. 'Now we just have to move in.'

I flip my menu open. Bryan says something about a French nouveau influence as I read a description of the Jelly Croque Madame—*thin slices of black forest ham with Dijon between two slices of scratch-made French toast, topped with an egg over easy.* The menu is a little more complicated than either of us was expecting, with a laundry list of crepe selections and experimental takes on eggs Benedict such as the Caprese Bennie and the Pot Roast Bennie.

'I don't know what to get,' Bryan says.

'They *do* make their own jelly here,' I say, eyes fixed on my menu. I'm amused. Bryan always knows what he wants—it's always the same thing. Bacon, two eggs sunny side, and wheat toast. He likes to jelly up his toast and dip it in egg yolk, much to my derision—'Jelly with eggs? Freak.'

If he's feeling fancy, he'll choose a seedless blackberry jam over his usual grape jelly—'Seedless is for pussies,' I'll say.

It never ceases to amaze me the kind of crap he eats, being a chef. He'll go from serving up an exquisite prime rib ('better than Gordon Ramsay's,' according to one of his regulars) to scarfing down nachos with pickle relish from a 7-Eleven. He'll braise a wild rabbit in white wine and pare a carrot down into a flower but turn around and order the same plain breakfast every day.

'New home, new prospects,' Bryan says. He flips the laminated page. 'Maybe I feel like trying something different.'

I fondle one of the daisies on our table as he hums a quiet tune and sips his coffee. Bryan says, 'Damn it, I still can't decide,' and I laugh. I tell him the orange juice sounds great, they squeeze it fresh. I ask what he thinks of a Tiffany-blue shower curtain for the new place. Maybe coral towels. I want to unpack right away. No more living out of boxes. I want to keep this place nice and tidy, track household chores on a calendar. Cook something from scratch once a week at least. Do everything right this time.

Bryan reaches across the table to take my hand. He says, 'Whatever you want, baby.'

The life cycle of *Cimex lectularius*, commonly known as the bedbug, begins with a pearl-white egg no bigger than the head of a pin. Once hatched, the bedbug goes through six molting stages that result in translucent skins sloughed discreetly behind baseboards, within mattresses, and in other cracks or crevices in proximity to the bug's host. At each stage, the bedbug must consume blood to shed its exoskeleton.

The female bedbug can lay three to four eggs each day for about nine months under warm conditions, and as many as five hundred eggs in its lifespan. A single pregnant survivor of eradication can be responsible for an entire infestation, rapidly producing generations of offspring.

The first day of our new lease, as the movers drive off, I let out a bloodcurdling scream. When Bryan dashes into the bedroom to check on me, I point out several fat bedbugs crawling lazily up the walls. We sleep on the couch that night.

I keep calling the office and they keep copping the same attitude like I'm a clingy girlfriend they're trying to dump. I know the preamble by heart: 'Hi, my name is Sung. We live in unit 17-205 and we've been corresponding about a pest control issue?' I've worked my share of pink-collar jobs. I know how to play it. But they're dragging ass on me. First they say we'll have our apartment assessed the next business day. It takes three for the inspector to get there. Days wasted just to confirm something we already know when we could be scheduling a treatment. It takes another week of phone tag to get a treatment on the books. The property managers haven't given up on convincing us we brought them in ourselves. When we remind them that we first encountered the bugs the day we moved in, they suggest that what we saw that day weren't bedbugs—maybe they were ticks or beetles. Any time we visit the leasing office to negotiate the issue, they take us into a private room away from potential tenants. They refuse to say the word *bedbug* out loud.

We're two weeks into our new lease and we haven't been able to unpack yet.

The EPA advises residents of an infested home to treat clothes and linens in a hot dryer for a minimum of thirty minutes, which will kill bedbugs and eggs. Washing alone may not be sufficient. Clean items should then be stored in airtight plastic bags to ensure they remain bug-free. Infested items should be quarantined and, if untreatable, disposed of. Eggs take several weeks to incubate and hatch—improper quarantine procedures may lead to re-infestation.

We drop the dog off with my parents. We take all of our towels, bedding, and clothes, seal them in garbage bags, and head to the laundromat. We spend almost fifty dollars washing and drying everything, and buying new bags to seal the clean clothes in. We heap diatomaceous earth along the baseboards, behind our mattress, between our couch cushions. We spray ourselves with rubbing alcohol before leaving the house just in case.

The exterminator sprays our apartment down. Fumes billow out our windows while we scrape eggs across our plate at the diner down the street. The bugs seem to be gone. The bites start healing. We stop living out of plastic bags. We bring the dog home. We start sleeping naked again.

Bryan slides the covers down to place his hand on my thigh. He says, 'I feel like we haven't had any time to be a couple.'

I remind him that we haven't exactly been alone. We laugh but his fingers tense and sink in. He pushes his face close and kisses me. Our breaths syncopate. I keep my eyes open to watch his features blur.

Sometimes it's hard not to look.

Sometimes you don't have to say everything.

I lean back as Bryan trails a finger between my breasts. He creeps under the blanket and buries his head between my knees.

My hips lurch wildly to the beat of his breath. My mouth wraps around those obscene half-words of a gluttonous, angry rapture. My eyes are wide open to the stinging sterile light of our bedroom with the powdered corners, our dresser still shrink-wrapped from the move.

At first, I'm not sure what I'm seeing. Then it stirs.

There's a bedbug on our ceiling. It's fat and ripened a nice raisin-brown with our blood.

'I love you,' Bryan says.

I watch the little parasite crawl slowly toward a wall.

'I love you too,' I say.

Sometimes you don't have to say everything.

The bedbug reproduces solely through a process called *traumatic insemination*, also known as *hypodermic insemination*. This is the mating practice in which the male pierces the female's abdomen and injects sperm through the puncture. This process creates an open wound that is susceptible to infection and impairs the female until it has healed.

Our next time at Jelly, the atmosphere feels different. The servers don't seem peppy, they seem rushed. The pastels no longer friendly but garish. The daisies feel overstated—maybe hydrangeas would suit the place better? Or wildflowers? Or maybe I'm being neurotic and fussy? We get the corner booth again and the squeak of the vinyl irritates me. I hate how the seat sticks to my thighs. Bryan rubs his temples. He barely looks at his menu before snapping it closed, hunching over his coffee mug with his shades still on. He furiously scratches a row of bites on his elbow, but quickly clears his throat and stuffs his hands in his pockets when one of the servers passes our table. He touches my foot under the table by accident, then quickly jerks away and mutters that he's sorry.

I take a deep breath and a sip of coffee. 'What are you getting?'

Bryan scans the dining room and anxiously chews at his cuticles.

We both know what he's getting. 'Bacon. Eggs sunny side. Wheat toast.'

After speaking with someone at the tenants' rights union, Bryan says it might be a good idea to have photographic evidence handy in case we have to prove something. So I take his phone and tell him to stand over here in the light.

He looks scrawny and ragged in his underwear, his eyes bulging with sleeplessness, his milky soft skin broken out in raised red patches. The pictures look strange and insidious. Disembodied shots of arms, legs, chest, back. A nipple here, a mole there. Framed at antiseptic angles in poor lighting. Something between a medical illustration and an unsolicited dick pic.

Bryan crouches, his back curved shyly like a half moon. He looks so small. I look at those angry rashes up and down his body and think of that old cliché, *don't let your clothes wear you.* He looks washed out, eclipsed, damn near consumed. I touch him here, a puffy patch of shoulder that radiates a dull heat. I touch him there, on his scabby shin with a dab of peppermint oil to cool the itch. I press a cold glass of water against his neck and he sighs softly. His face twists with embarrassment.

Two months into our lease and there are still boxes stacked to the ceiling, dimming the light with their imposing silhouette. We sit around slumped and defeated in the heat as the TV chatters quietly, our ravaged bodies side by side, naked and vulnerable. I watch his ruddy wounds weep pus and glisten with salve. I lay my hand against him carelessly. I don't watch where I touch. I don't care where I kiss.

The exterminator is waiting for us out front when we get back. He packs away his gas mask, clearing his throat like there's something stuck in it. Bryan and I walk up together, holding hands like a normal couple having a normal morning.

I look up at the apartment. The windows are fogged up, like a storm is brewing inside. I ask what we can do to help ensure the treatment's efficacy. I mention how a friend suggested dabbing lavender oil near the bed because bugs hate it.

'There's no such thing as a preventative treatment,' the exterminator says. He adjusts his cap and shakes his head. 'If the office tells you different, don't listen. Don't listen to anything they have to say. People want the problem to stay quiet, you know? They want you to think it's your own fault. They'll tell you all kinds of stuff.'

I watch the dense gray haze through our windows up on the second floor. Bryan squeezes my hand.

'They might always come back,' the exterminator says. 'You never know they're really gone until you move out. If they do come back, call me as soon as you notice. It's all you can really do.'

We thank him, but he's quick to dismiss our gratitude with a humble shake of the head. The problem is bigger than he can solve. It's bigger than our unit, our building, our neighborhood. It's bigger than pest control.

Bryan's hand slinks up my back like a long breath. He watches me squint up at our apartment in the unrelenting heat.

It's July. There's a dead bird in the entryway. I start laughing and I can't stop.

The bedbug's flat body and nimble legs allow it to creep into narrow spaces such as between a wall and baseboard, in the seams of bookshelves, and behind electrical outlets. It can fit into any space that will accommodate a credit card. As the bedbug is largely a nocturnal species, residents of infested buildings may never encounter them in the day. An afflicted individual may wake up with itchy bites in rows or clusters, never the wiser to their source. These bites are frequently mistaken for flea bites, scabies, or simply allergic reactions, even by doctors. It is impossible to diagnose a bedbug infestation by the bites alone.

One evening we're bickering. I'm needling him. Bryan grits his teeth and clamps down until he snaps. His voice shoots up like a geyser, like a rifle. I thrash against the doorway. I am screaming. My hand is open and it connects. Things go flying. Things keep falling. I am screaming until I am whispering, 'No, no, please.' He tries to come close but I am screaming. I curl up under a table begging, 'No, please, stop.' I am beating my open hands against my ears, eyes shut tight. My heart pounds like war. I don't know where I am.

It takes a long time to feel Bryan's hands locked around my wrists. 'Please don't do that,' he says.

It takes a long time to realize I've been hitting myself.

I open my eyes. There are broken things everywhere. Bryan looks down at the cracked remnants of the ceramic bowl we kept our keys in. He stacks the shards in an open hand and dumps them in the trash. He vacuums up the splinters we can't see.

'My old teacher gave that to me,' he says quietly. 'He made it almost twenty years ago.'

My eyes well up again. 'I didn't mean to break it,' I say. 'I don't know what happened. I'm so sorry.'

'Don't be sorry,' he says. 'It's just stuff.'

He kneels next to me where the bowl broke and puts his hand over my head. He wraps me up in his arms. He says it again and again. *It's just stuff.*

Reactions to bedbug bites vary greatly from person to person. For some, rashes may take several days to develop, while others might show signs of inflammation within hours. Some do not display any symptoms whatsoever.

When irritated by way of scratching, an area of inflammation typically grows larger. It may therefore seem that the bites are spreading or multiplying, even after a full course of treatment has eradicated the infestation.

Months after the exterminator has cleared our unit, Bryan and I are lounging in bed when I feel something brush against my neck. I shriek, batting at myself with my eyes shut tight. I don't realize I'm still screaming until Bryan claps a hand on my shoulder and shakes me.

'What's wrong?'

'The bugs are back.'

He thinks a moment.

Then he takes my hand and says, 'That was my hair.'

As our lease dwindles to its final weeks, Bryan and I alternate between bickering over nothing in particular and uneasy laughter. Every once in awhile we joke about the possibility of bedbugs in the new place. 'Chicago's one of the bedbug hotspots of the world,' Bryan says. We laugh about it but not without some tart apprehension. We've taken to calling our current apartment 'The Bedbug Palace.' The property managers are asking for an additional hundred bucks a month if we choose to stay here. The entire year we've lived here, they've been advertising a nonexistent bowling alley on a big sign by the leasing office that says COMING SOON.

I wrap a ceramic plate with a foam sheet and hand it to Bryan. 'I still want to set that goddamn leasing office on fire,' I say. 'Piss on their porch.'

Bryan laughs as he stacks the plate in a box on the floor. 'I still want to spray-paint BEDBUGS all over the buildings,' he says.

I remind him of the time he threatened to bag up the bugs and set them loose in the property management office.

He reminds me of the time I stomped in there with my boots on yelling about bedbugs until three potential tenants slunk out, horrified.

'Bryan, if we get bedbugs again, I really might start bombing federal buildings,' I say.

He says, 'I'm right there with you, man.'

I wake up late, naked, and alone.

It takes a long time to remember where I am. I'm still learning the layout of our new apartment and for a moment I can't tell *when* I am. Is this today? Is this last year? Is this the future?

The sink is running in the bathroom. I toss the covers off and lie there feeling stretched out and heavy for a while. Starting from the neck, I work my hands down my body in swift elliptical sweeps. It takes a while to realize I am checking for bug bites. I roll out of bed and shuffle down the hall into the new living room. There are cardboard boxes stacked high against the walls. Grit tickles the soles of my feet.

The sink is running in the bathroom but I don't call Bryan's name. I don't look for my phone.

A hard breeze pushes through the open windows, carrying the smell of grass and damp concrete. I stand in a hot white slice of sunlight watching dust dance. My muscles rise like bread in the warmth.

During my trip to Portland in the last stages of writing this book, I keep to myself as much as I can aside from meetings with my publisher and a few trips to the convenience store for a pack of smokes and hard-boiled eggs. Vonn comes with me and we are almost immediately set on edge. It's not a city we feel safe or right in. I'm smacked in the face with the fact of my complicity each time a homeless man howls something lewd my way because I'm wearing a tight dress and no bra. The thing is he's not invading my space. I'm walking through his. That is where he lives.

It doesn't upset me. My position in the world and its possibility upsets me.

I am not affronted by these aggressions. I am disgusted with a world in which they are a last resort of the downtrodden.

I am not scared of being robbed by someone in need. I am scared of what white supremacists may be among those mean-mugging me as I pass by.

I see the whitest people I have ever seen in Portland. I see more happy dogs and homeless people than I have ever seen in Portland. I'm dizzied by the gentrified sprawl of this place. The weed dispensaries and the culture around them perfectly sum up the libertarian nightmare this place personifies to me—white people who love compost and dogs but hate the homeless and black people. I have no business being here. I feel sick. Our first night here, Vonn and I hold each other and cry on the porch about being stared at by all these scary white people, about what family means for people like us under white supremacy, about our helplessness in the face of such deeply ingrained economic injustice.

But eventually we get stir-crazy and visit some tourist traps. We wander into one of those hippie stores run by nice bougie white ladies in long hand-dyed linens. It's hard to deny that this ambiance is soothing after a week of feeling jarred raw by our surroundings—the shitty easy-listening music on the PA, the waft of nag champa, the way these nice white ladies speak in voices soft as sand. I give in to it. I handle shiny crystals, sift through powdery cones of incense. I tap my foot to Yanni. I pick out an ornate thumb piano with a sticker that reads MADE IN INDONESIA for Bryan and have it bubble-wrapped at the counter. I am literally wearing a fanny pack that says CHICAGO.

We are trying to acclimate. We are trying to have a normal day. It's not ethical. It's not right. It's just what we sometimes do.

When I get home from Portland, I immediately strip off my pants and lie back on my couch. Leroy frantically nuzzles my side and I sit there holding her, sticky with flop sweat and exhausted. My face feels greasy from the plane ride home and my throat is scorched from a weeklong cigarette binge that I have no intention of telling Bryan about. I tell Bryan I have something for him and he sits next to me. I hand him the bubble-wrapped thumb piano and watch him unwrap it with great care, peeling the tape back and everything.

He holds the instrument up and watches light travel down its glossy wooden body. He turns it over, examines it from every angle. He plucks its metal tines one by careful one, tries chords, a simple little melody. He hugs it close and smiles as he thanks me. His face looks so open in the tight amber glow of our apartment, all his little nooks snagging shadows. This discovery. This uncomplicated pleasure, the flick of a thumb, a mellow sound to the ear, the stringing together of a song.

I think about the times I've watched Bryan pick up a standing bass on stage at an open mic. Swaying side to side and plucking those fretless strings with that easy energy, like locking into an embrace when you've missed somebody. I think about the last time he picked up a paintbrush and all the effort it took for him to crawl out from under the crushing weight of a world that won't value its strokes. I think about a life where he doesn't have to spend eight hours a day explaining expensive deli meats to nice white ladies who ask if it's nitrite-free or gluten-free or preservative-free, nice white ladies who complain about his store running out of potato salad like he brings the potatoes from home himself, nice white ladies who ask his coworker at the sushi bar if they can have sushi without rice. Nice white ladies who bring back a hunk of cheese that costs more than our last trip to the grocery store because it's sliced too thick. I think about how every single day, he handles more money than he'll ever have.

I think about a life where all he has to worry about is being himself. Where a moment of joy, of catharsis, of discovery, like this one, is ever nearer.

And I want to enjoy this moment in a room away from the world. I want this moment contained. I don't want to know about the Indonesian sweatshop this thumb piano came from, the Shona people of Zimbabwe who've seen nothing of the profits yielded by their innovation. I don't want to think about those white ladies plundering whole continents by proxy to run their little boutiques, or especially the fact that they're doing it with my money. But that room can't exist in an open heart. You can't live in that room and feel the lurch of human struggle at the same time. Those white ladies, they give that part of themselves up. They don't wonder where the shit they peddle comes from, *really* comes from, the human cost of our lifestyles. They turn away, and they don't experience the fullest potential of wonder.

I watch the man I love work his calloused hands over this gift. This fragile possibility.

He makes me want to burn down banks.

He makes me want to kill the president and bomb the FDA.

date: Sat, July 8, 2017 at 8:15 PM
subject: Photos

[redacted],

This is Sung.

I'm not even sure this is the right email address, and if so, whether or not it's still active.

I hope you're well. I don't know how you feel about me or how we left things in retrospect. I don't want to revisit any of that. I don't want to rehash anything painful or upset either of our lives by contacting you. It's just that you're the last person to have seen my childhood photos. I still don't believe you destroyed them--I never really thought you'd do that. If you do have them stashed somewhere, I wonder if you'd give them back. Send them through the mail to me, maybe.

The photo of me on my birthday, my grandmother took that and she won't be around forever. It's the only happy birthday I ever had as a child.

Those are the only photos I've ever had where I'm smiling.

If they're still in your home somewhere, please consider returning them to me. After all that hurt and anguish, I'm not bitter or angry with you. That's all I want from you, those pictures. I do hope you're well.

Best,

S

date: Mon, July 10, 2017 at 9:14 AM
subject: RE: Photos

Sung, good to hear from you.

I do not believe I have those pics, I am sorry to say.

I was surprised to receive your email, and thinking about it all, I have to say, I want to take you over my knee and spank you hard like a bad little girl. If I did, there would be real anger, and real pain involved, I think.

You are welcome to come over and help me look for them, except I don't think you will find them.

I know my truth.

Our window refracts the sapphire glow of midnight, diffusing it in a wash of gray shadows over us. I am sitting up in bed, my breath a rustling, untamed chill. Bryan's hand explores my back, as if looking for a button or drawstring. I don't know what's wrong besides everything. There is just too much. I'm in the last stretch of my manuscript. Graduation is next week. Then I fly to Portland to meet with people about my book when it's not even finished. I am embarrassed that I still have problems. That I've written a memoir without even getting over these problems. I felt like the closing of this book really would be the closing of this book—like the writing was supposed to be a kind of healing unto itself. I was supposed to emerge fully transformed after typing THE END, the kinda bitch who can take long, confident strides into a Chipotle and rattle off an order without stuttering or saying sorry even once. The kinda bitch who never cancels plans because of an unexpected meltdown. The kinda bitch who can get showered and dressed without putting it on a to-do list.

But I'm still here. Still me. Still unemployed. Still rocking in place and struggling to speak through this frenetic sobbing. I need Bryan to look me in the eyes. I need him to hold me. Tether me to this room. To my skin. To this night. I need, I need, I need, but I can't bring myself to ask. I curl around myself and turn away.

For the longest time Bryan's little affirmations hang suspended in the air. His voice like a wisp of cloud, like breath pushing in and out and stacking gently in the space around us. 'You are not worthless.' 'You give more than you know.' 'You're beautiful.' I hear him and I don't know what's happening to me. I don't know how it happens but it finally does. We connect. He runs the back of his hand against my cheek, a whisper of touch. He is looking into my eyes and suddenly this breakdown feels silly.

Leroy hijacks my pillow and unleashes a ripe fart that wafts right into Bryan's face. We laugh quietly, so quietly, like the moment is a fragile little eggshell that could be broken apart just by noise. Bryan closes his eyes and I shift onto my side to look at him.

'I don't think I can stay up much longer,' he says.

I tell him he doesn't have to.

'Are you sure you're okay?'

I rest my hand on his chest. Just to touch him. To get another little taste of what he feels like because I can. He moans softly, sleepily, the sound light as down. I wrap my hand around his throat.

'Do you remember sleeping like this?' I say.

'Yeah, I remember,' he says. 'I've never let anyone else do that.'

'What do you mean?'

I feel his pulse in my fingers. Or my pulse in his throat.

'Anyone else tried that,' he mumbles, 'I'd probably . . . be very quick to . . . I might hurt them.'

He is drifting quickly now. His voice garbled by sleep.

'Why let me do it then?' I ask.

He hooks his arm around mine, securing my cupped hand around his throat as he rolls onto his side.

'Why?' I ask again.

He snorts and smacks his lips. 'I must love you,' he says. 'I must trust you.'

This is the wrong time to think of Pauly but I do. I think of all those times we would lie back in his king size bed after I let him fuck me raw with his eyes closed. I would lean my head against his neck and run my fingers through those coarse, graying chest hairs. He would take my wrist and click his tongue as if to control the wandering curiosity of a dog. He would hold my wrist suspended like that, my arm stretched in the air like a bridge between us. He would say, 'Not the heart baby.' He would say, 'Don't touch my heart.' He would say, 'How many times have I told you.'

I remember being charmed by this. I remember being charmed by his temper, his drinking problem, his strange and rigid rules, his abuse. It made him elusive. Interesting. I thought that was love. I thought accepting the hurt he doled out and writing vague, lyrical poems about it was love. I thought accepting hurt was the only way I could get close enough to be maybe, hopefully, loved.

Love is not a white lie. It doesn't fill the cracks and make bad things beautiful or okay. Love is allowing ourselves to be fooled, not being fooled. Leaving ourselves open to hurt, not the hurt itself. Leaving ourselves open to delusion, not delusion itself. It's not a guarantee, it's the act of promising. The breathtaking act of hope. It's the stupid high-stakes gamble that pays off. It's a whisper of touch. It's a window flung open and naked to the day.

Sung Yim

Yesterday at 2:01 p.m. · Chicago, IL ·

u should have at least 6 favorite paintings and 7 films that changed u. 13 poems that saved ur life. 700 songs that make u feel a thing. a list of reasons why u like a brand of cereal or toothpaste. u should whittle. u should jack off. u should think about flowers. u should listen to people.

ACKNOWLEDGMENTS

Special thanks are due to the Perfect Day Publishing team: editor Jessie Carver for her quick eye and unexpectedly loving feedback, Aaron Miller for the striking cover design and for putting up with my fussy standards, and of course Michael Heald for giving me a chance at such a crucial time of my life, and pushing me to finally sew my wounds back up like a big boy. Thank you also to the brilliant Luther Hughes, who has always generously shared the wealth, and without whom Michael might never have found my work.

Thank you to editors Corinne Manning, Elissa Washuta, Jeff McMahon, Timothy Green, Caseyrenée Lopez, and especially the tender-hearted Laura Pegram, all of whom created spaces in which my vision could thrive.

Thank you to the faculty members of Columbia College Chicago, among those: Jenny Boully, whose innovative genius taught me the value of starting over; T Clutch Fleischmann, whose warmth and valiant example as an artist gave me the courage to be my weird self on paper; David MacLean, who rightly saw through my aversion to compliments; Re'Lynn Hansen, who finessed my senioritis with great sensitivity and grace; and CM Burroughs, whose sharp critique snapped me out of my poor judgment during a time when I should have known better, and whose reading list unmistakably changed my life.

Thank you to Anne Davidovicz and Nancy Davis at Harper College, the first people who taught me how to let words into my heart and who gave me my start as a writer in huge ways.

Thank you to Glenn Taylor, who set a crucial standard for how I should expect to be treated by men in positions of power early on—which is to say, with appropriate and unwavering respect—and whose subtle affirmation paved the way for things I always imagined but never imagined could actually happen.

My deepest gratitude to Siobhan Roca Thompson, who shaped the outcome of this book with her incisive revision notes and who admittedly taught me how to hug like a normal person, as well as all the beautiful, freakish, gifted friends I've made in Chicago, most of whom have saved my life on occasion.

Most of all, heartfelt thanks to Bryan Park for lending me his actual name in the oft-ignominious telling of our story, for understanding the ruthless drive of an artist better than anyone, for the promise of following me anywhere, and for putting up, and putting up, and putting up with the exhausting reality of what's enclosed within this book.

Sung Yim is a bilingual South Korean immigrant living in Illinois. Their essays and poems have appeared in *The James Franco Review, Contrary, Kweli, Crab Fat Magazine,* and in a chapbook from Ghost City Press.